WHY DOES BEING A CHRISTIAN HAVE TO BE SO HARD?

Studies in Hebrews 12:1-13

WHY DOES BEING A CHRISTIAN HAVE TO BE SO HARD?

Studies in Hebrews 12:1-13

by

Peter E. Golding

 EVANGELICAL PRESS

EVANGELICAL PRESS
Faverdale North Industrial Estate, Darlington, DL3 0PH,
England

Evangelical Press USA
P. O. Box 825, Webster, New York 14580, USA

e-mail: sales@evangelicalpress.org

web: http://www.evangelicalpress.org

First published 2004

British Library Cataloguing in Publication Data available

ISBN 0 85234 578X

Printed and bound in Great Britain by CPD (Wales),
Ebbw Vale

To Hilary,
steadfast in adversity.

And to the members and friends
at Hayes Town Chapel, past and present.

Contents

1 Keep on Keeping on! (verse 1)   13

2 The Only Way (verse 2)   23

3 The Christian's Fainting-Fits (verses 3-4)   35

4 Consider Him! (verses 2-3)   46

5 Spiritual Amnesia (verses 5-6)   57

6 Sonship (verses 5-6)   68

7 Son-Training (verses 5-6)   79

8 Losing Heart (verses 5-6)   90

9 Responding to Discipline (verses 5-9)   102

10 Chastisement – Human and Divine (verses 7-10)   113

11 Harvest Time (verses 10-11)   124

12 A Spiritual Work-Out (verses 12-13)   134

Notes   144

Foreword

Discipline is a harsh sounding word. Change the final letter to 'g' and you have discipling. That is more user friendly but no less serious. Jesus became a disciple though He was God's own son, and it was for our eternal benefit. How much more do we who are sinners, but who have been adopted by His Father, need to be taught to please Him! These messages will be of immense help towards that great goal.

Dr. Hywel R. Jones
Professor of Practical Theology
Westminster Theological Seminary
Escondido, California

Preface

These chapters had their genesis in twelve expository sermons preached at Hayes Town Chapel, Middlesex in 1993-4. They were preached in connection with pastoral needs in the congregation, and in particular the personal adversities through which the author and his family were passing at the time.

The only reason that can possibly justify publishing these addresses in this revised format is the pressure brought to bear by friends who heard them, together with the desire that God may be pleased to use them to 'succour those who are being tried.'

I would like to express my sincere gratitude to Albert Peters, onetime staff worker with the Lord's Day Observance Society, without whose friendship and advice these studies would never have seen the light of day. His suggestions and work in correcting and preparing the text have been invaluable.

Peter E. Golding
Wraxall, North Somerset, 2004

1 | keep on keeping on!

'Therefore, since we are surrounded by such a great cloud of witnesses, let us throw off everything that hinders and the sin that so easily entangles, and let us run with perseverance the race marked out for us.'

Hebrews 12:1

Before considering this passage in detail it is essential to know something of the background against which this letter was written.

Its author, whose identity we do not know for sure, wrote to these Jewish believers because he was clearly very concerned about their spiritual state. Consequently, he was anxious to strengthen them in the faith and to comfort and encourage them at what was obviously a very difficult and trying time in their lives.

But as a wise physician of the soul, he did not flatter these people. He did not tell them that everything was fine and therefore not to worry. Rather, the writer knew that in order to give them true comfort, he must do so in terms of their real condition, which gave him considerable cause for concern, not to say alarm.

Discouraged

It seems clear that many of these Hebrew Christians had become discouraged and fainthearted, largely because of the persecution and trials they were undergoing. For the same reason many of them were grumbling and complaining about their lot. However, as a result of all this, and most serious of all, some were beginning to look back with longing eyes to the old life of Judaism in which they had been born and nurtured, but from which they had been saved and delivered. According to the writer to the Hebrews there is nothing more fearful and dangerous than that, because, as he himself puts it in chapter ten verse thirty-nine, to go back from God's final revelation in the Lord Jesus Christ is to go back to destruction.

Although the writer wants to help these folk and console them, he must bear in mind the perilous condition they were in, and the temptation to which this exposed them. So as we read through this tremendous epistle, we find that one of its most characteristic features is the way in which we get these alternating passages of warning on the one hand and yet of encouragement on the other. This pattern is very evident in this twelfth chapter.

Jesus the Mediator

If the writer does not encourage these struggling saints he knows it will lead to depression. But being realistic, he also knows that if he does not admonish and exhort them it will lead to presumption. So wisely he does both. There is one basic charge though that he has to level at his readers. He points out that all their troubles and difficulties can ultimately be traced back to one thing: they had failed to grasp the *superiority* and the utter *finality* of the Christian message, as revealed in Jesus the Mediator of the New Covenant. All their problems stemmed from the failure of these people to keep their eyes fixed firmly on this blessed person.

Rather, they were looking at their tribulations and their afflictions. Like the Apostle Peter, when the Lord encouraged him to walk to him on the water, they could only look at the waves – at the sea of troubles that seemed about to engulf them. And like Peter, they were starting to sink. There was only one way to put them right: they urgently needed to be reminded of Jesus their great High Priest, who, as verse two reminds us, 'for the joy set before him endured the cross, scorning its shame.'

Similar situation

In passing, there is no doubt that we are in a very similar situation. One of the greatest problems at the present time is that of discouragement. As we see what is happening in the world, with its abounding sin, and as we consider the situation in the church, the temptation is to feel downhearted, even hopeless about it all. On top of that are those personal trials and setbacks that are the lot of all of us in this life. The thought comes to us: 'why go on? What is the point of it all?'

Although that is a perfectly natural reaction it is not the spiritual way to respond to these things – and for this reason: all such gloom and despondency stems from a failure to grasp the greatness of the Christian message and the glory of Christ.

The solemn reality is that once a professing Christian begins to question the ways of God, perhaps even to query his love, that person is in imminent danger of falling away and apostatizing from the faith – hence the seriousness with which the writer addresses this issue.

The link

Clearly, chapter twelve follows on immediately from the close of chapter eleven. So, in order to view the opening verses of chapter twelve in their context and setting, we need to establish the link with what has gone before. In the eleventh chapter the writer is dealing with the nature of saving faith, and the fruit it invariably brings forth in the lives of true Christians.

He does this by way of illustration from the lives of numerous Old Testament saints. 'By faith Abel offered God a better sacrifice than Cain...by faith Enoch was taken from this life...' and so on, right through the old dispensation. It is as if we are being conducted round a portrait gallery, with our guide pausing in front of each picture, and recounting to us how by faith this particular hero of the faith did what he did. The connection with chapter twelve is this: having displayed the character and evidences of faith from those representative examples, the writer now applies it to his readers.

This is why the chapter opens with the word 'therefore'. It means 'in the light of', or 'in view of', indicating that he is making a deduction from what he has just been saying and arriving at certain conclusions. Having fully illustrated his teaching on faith by that detailed and eloquent survey of Old Testament history, he now urges us to work out its implications in our own lives. Let us follow him as he does so.

THE NECESSITY OF PERSEVERANCE

> *'Therefore… let us run with perseverance the race marked out for us…'* (verse 1).

The writer's great aim is to encourage these Hebrews to go on in the Christian life, and not to go back as some had done. But he does so by using a powerful and imaginative figure of speech – that of running a race. As it has often been pointed out, when the New Testament pictures the Christian life as a race, it has in mind not so much the one hundred metres sprint but the marathon. However, that is not all here. Keeping this idea of a race in his mind's eye, the writer develops the illustration, and, in a very wonderful way, links it with that magnificent review of the heroes of the faith that he had just given.

Cloud of witnesses

> *'Therefore, since we are surrounded by such a great cloud of witnesses…'* (verse 1).

It is a graphic picture he paints. Doubtless what he had in mind was the great public games, the forerunner of our modern Olympic games, staged by the Greeks at that time in honour of Jupiter. It is the picture of a race run in a vast stadium, in which the runners are surrounded by crowds of spectators cheering them on. Obviously, this refers to the multitude of believers who have gone before, who lived and died in faith; examples of whom we have just been given. What the writer is saying is this: 'Look, you have started well, but the race is not over yet, the prize is not yet gained. And lest any of you should be tempted to give up in discouragement, remember that you are not alone in this. Countless others have gone before and won through. They were once where you are now, struggling in the arena. But by faith they persevered and gained the prize, and so too must you.'

Is there someone reading this who is flagging and is tempted to drop out? What you need to realize is that you are not alone in the struggle. Go back! Look at the long history of the Church down the centuries, and there you will see a great cloud of witnesses whose very example urges us all on, shouting their encouragements as with one voice: 'Run in such a way as to get the prize!' (1 Cor. 9:24).

I press on

This illustration of the life of faith as akin to a race is a very common one in the New Testament, especially in the writings of Paul. For instance, the apostle puts it like this in his letter to the Philippians: '...But one thing I do: Forgetting what is behind and straining towards what is ahead, I press on towards the goal to win the prize for which God has called me heavenwards in Christ Jesus' (Phil. 3:13-14). To reach heaven and glory, I have got to run for it!

According to this teaching, there is an inseparable connection between running the race and receiving the prize. Persevering in faith, holiness, and obedience to the revealed will of God in Scripture, is not an optional extra, but an indispensable necessity to the attainment of final salvation. The Lord himself was emphatic on this. It is '...he who stands firm to the end will be saved' (Matt. 24:13) – and we can add, *only* he. It is not the person who starts well, or the one who endures for a time, who will be saved. It is he who continues and completes the course.

Why is the Christian life pictured as running a race? The explanation is this. One of the most terrible effects of the Fall and of sin is to make us careless and casual about the things that matter most, while allowing us to become engrossed and obsessive about the things that matter hardly at all. The truth is, says the writer to the Hebrews, that if there is no *running*, there will be no *winning* – it is impossible to gain the prize without finishing the course!

Ignorance

This is a simple, even obvious point to make, and yet it must be made because ignorance of this principle, even among evangelical Christians, is quite staggering. People say; 'Oh yes, I expect to be in heaven,' when in reality the only reason they have for saying it is that they just cannot imagine themselves going to hell! But speak to them of perseverance in holiness, 'without which no one will see the Lord' (verse fourteen), and one would imagine you were suffering from religious fanaticism. Such people want the result – the prize of eternal life – but they want it without the arduous slog of running that alone will lead to that result. However you cannot have the one without the other. There will be no prize in the world *to come* if one is a stranger to perseverance in *this* world, with all that this entails. The rule has no exceptions.

INTENSITY IN PERSEVERANCE

By this very metaphor of the Christian life as a race, we are being told a great deal about the character of this wonderful life: a life that is so great and glorious, and so many-sided, that no one illustration can ever do justice to it. However, one thing that is clear is that just as a race involves the participants in strenuous and intense exertion, so too does the spiritual demands of the life of faith.

Also we need to bear in mind that this is not simply the concentrated exertion necessary to run the hundred metres sprint, but the patient, consistent effort required in the marathon. This is one reason why, with so great a salvation freely offered, and with such a wonderful prize to be gained, that so few, relatively speaking, have entered the race. They have counted the cost and found it too high. As G.K. Chesterton once put it, 'Christianity has not been tried and found wanting, it has been found too difficult and not tried.'

That is why even these Jewish Christians were so sorely tempted to give up and revert to Judaism. Anyone can *start* well in a race, and, if one is reasonably fit, complete the first few laps with comparitive ease. But it is a different matter when the other runners start forcing the pace. Then, even when your legs feel like lead, your lungs feel like bursting, and you have 'hit the wall'; as the modern vernacular has it, you have still got to go on – there is no let-up. How important it is to realize this. Granted, no one is finally saved on the basis or grounds of their perseverance. That is salvation by works. And yet no one is saved apart from, or without perseverance – and that is not just playing with words! Professor John Murray states it perfectly in his valuable little book, *Redemption Accomplished and Applied*: 'We do not attain to the prize of the high calling of God in Christ automatically. Perseverance means the engagement of our persons in the most intense and concentrated devotion to those means which God has ordained for the achievement of his saving purpose.'[1] Indeed, the very term 'perseverance' implies that.

A simple illustration will make the point. If you were on holiday and had the opportunity to get up late each morning, you would not write a postcard home saying that you had *persevered* in having a lie-in every morning. No! – for the very good reason that relaxation comes too easily to be described in that way. You see the point!

Going on

It is likely, if not probable, that you would not be reading these words if you did not make *some* Christian profession. But the crucial issue is this: Are you persevering in the Christian life? Are you going on? Or are you falling behind in the race? Are you the kind of person referred to in Proverbs 21:25? 'The desire of the slothful killeth him…' (KJV). Why does his desire kill him? It is because this person never gets round to doing something about it. They are always promising themself that one day they really will buckle down to living the Christian life, really will get down to Bible reading and prayer and faithful attendance at the means of grace. But somehow they never actually get round to it.

This is why the Apostle Paul was so concerned with the Galatians. 'You were running a good race' he says – what has hindered you? (5:7). This was so serious a matter that the apostle says this in chapter four, verse eleven: 'I fear for you, that somehow I have wasted my efforts on you.' May this never be said of us.

ACTIVITY IN PERSEVERANCE

According to John Murray, continuance in the faith involves 'the engagement of our whole persons in the most intense and concentrated devotion to those *means* that God has ordained for the achievement of his saving purpose.' What are those means? Happily for us, the writer to the Hebrews deals with this very matter as part of his extended metaphor of the Christian life as a race. He puts it in these words: 'Therefore…let us throw off everything that hinders, and the sin that so easily entangles.'

He is reminding us that the only way to run a race with any hope of winning is by discarding everything that might hold us back and impede our progress. That is so transparent in the natural realm that it hardly needs to be said, it is so self-evident. It *ought* to be equally clear in the realm of the Spirit. Tragically, however, the impression given in some circles is that so long as a person has 'decided for Christ', and believed 'the simple gospel', it is possible to get to heaven hanging on to all the bag and baggage of sin imaginable, even though that person might lose his 'reward'.

Stripping off

But the Bible does not teach that, because as John Murray says elsewhere, 'it sets up an impossible combination of things.' No! The Scriptural teaching is that there will be no final perseverance apart from the means that God has ordained for the achievement of his saving purpose. And that means stripping off everything that hinders, and the sin that so easily entangles.

If you attend an athletics meeting, or watch it on television, you expect the runners to strip down to the minimum. No one even keeps a tracksuit on, let alone their everyday clothing. It is exactly the same principle in the Christian life.

Coming to the particulars, what needs to be laid aside is put under two headings: *hindrances*, and *sins*. There is a very real sense in which the first of these two needs to be emphasized the most, for the following reason.

Most, if not all of us, realize that deliberate, continuous indulgence in sin that is not repented of, will keep us out of heaven. But we so often forget that there are many things in life which are not sinful *per se*, but which, if they control and dominate us, and obsess our thought-life, can hold us back just as surely, albeit more *deceptively*, as the most terrible of overt sins. It can be almost anything: interest in the other sex, sport, entertainment – even anxious cares and worries – it is all included. The list is almost endless. It comes to this. Is there in us that disposition of heart, which says, 'By the grace and help of God, I will endeavour to have done with everything that is calculated to impede my progress and hold me back in my Christian life, whatever the cost.' According to C.H. Spurgeon, 'darling sins must go first, for these, as they are the most loved, will have the most power to hinder.' It is a great test of where we stand.

THE POSSIBILITY OF PERSEVERANCE

And we need that encouragement. The writer exhorts us to run the race, not to mock us with vain and delusive hopes, but to urge us on with the certainty of success. This is borne out by the reference to this 'great cloud of witnesses' who have gone before, and are now in glory. Not only that, but we, at the beginning of the twenty-first century, are surrounded by that great 'cloud of witnesses' we read of in the New Testament and the subsequent annals of church history. We think of 'the noble army of martyrs', the Reformers, the Puritans, the Covenanters, the early Methodists, and a countless number of believers in every age. Their names may not appear in any book, but they ran the race with perseverance.

> A noble army, men and boys,
> The matron and the maid,
> Around the Saviour's throne rejoice,
> In robes of light arrayed.
> They climbed the steep ascent of heaven
> Through peril, toil, and pain;
> O God, to us may grace be given
> To follow in their train.
>
> *Reginald Heber*

There is only one way to do so. It is by fixing our eyes on Jesus, who has led the way. 'I can do all things through Christ...'

2 | the only way

Let us fix our eyes on Jesus, the author and perfecter of our faith, who for the joy set before him endured the cross, scorning its shame, and sat down at the right hand of the throne of God.'

Hebrews 12:2

It seems clear that many of those to whom this letter was originally addressed had become utterly dispirited in the Christian life, largely because of the trials they were being called on to endure. In particular they were undergoing militant persecution for the faith, even from their own fellow countrymen.

Like us, only in a more acute sense, these early Christians had no idea what a day might bring forth. They not only lived from day to day, but almost from moment to moment. Humanly speaking, the future was dark and full of uncertainty. Not surprisingly, these things were testing and trying their faith to the very limits. They could not understand why God was allowing all this to happen, and also could not reconcile it with the Gospel they had come to believe.

Why Lord?

But the Bible not only recognizes and takes account of our problems; it deals with them. There are times in all our lives when we cannot help but cry out, 'Why Lord? Why have you permitted these troubles and heartaches? What is the purpose of it all, if any?' We are faced with the perplexity of how to harmonize these things with a loving heavenly Father who cares for his children, and is concerned for their highest and best interests. But God knows this, and he has not left us to ourselves in our predicament. He understands the position; 'for he knows how we are formed, he remembers that we are dust.' (Psalm 103:14). So there is no need for us to try and work up some artificial comfort for ourselves, for the Lord has already provided this for us his Word, and especially in this section.

As a consequence of their distress some of these people were beginning to look back with wistful eyes to the old life of Judaism in which they had been born and nurtured, but out of which they had been saved and delivered by faith in Jesus as the promised Messiah.

Finally and completely

According to the writer to the Hebrews, there is nothing quite as dangerous to the soul as nostalgically looking back to the past. Those eloquent words at the very commencement of the letter tell us that although God *has* spoken in the past through the prophets, (and still speaks to us today through their writings in Scripture), he has spoken *finally* and *completely* by his Son, the Lord Jesus Christ. He is God's last and final word to the people. In him the divine revelation is fulfilled and completed. So to go back from God's final revelation in this blessed person is to go back to destruction, because there is nothing to go back to. Christ has superseded it all. No wonder the writer was alarmed. So, because of concern for his readers, he helps and encourages them, and provides incentives to 'keep on keeping on' in their Christian lives.

But as a faithful pastor and under-shepherd, he knows that sympathy and soothing expressions are not enough. That is what we all *like*, – and that is what we tend to think we *need*. Life in this world is never easy, and there are times when it can seem very cruel. The answer is never to hold a 'pity-party' for ourselves, and this man knew that. Sometimes the physician of the soul needs to be 'cruel to be kind', as we say, in order to keep us from this fatal tendency to self-pity. We rarely know what is best for us, but our heavenly Father does – hence those times in our experience when, although we think our great need is comfort, he knows that we need a stern word of rebuke as well. Verse five and following makes this very clear.

Not alone

However, the writer's great aim is to encourage his readers to persevere in the Christian life, and to warn them of the grave consequences of going back to the old life. He does so in verse one with an illustration that would surely stick like a burr in the memory. There, the life of faith is portrayed as a race run in a vast stadium: a race in which the contestants are surrounded by a great crowd of spectators, urging them on with their applause. It is a picture of the men and women of faith who have gone before us, and completed the course successfully.

The Christian who is weary and tired in the race, and wonders whether he will ever make it, must realize that he is not alone in the struggle. Go back, says this writer, and survey the past, and there the history of the people of God provides a glorious amphitheatre from which ten thousand times ten thousand voices cheer you on, as it were, all crying with one voice, 'so run, that you too may obtain!'

Perseverance and faith

For reasons that will become clear it is important that verses one and two should be taken together, and not isolated from each other. So before considering our text in more detail, we need first to look at verses one and two in general terms, and note the vital link between perseverance and faith.

The clear teaching of Scripture is that, just as there is an inseparable connection between running a race and gaining the prize, so according to the analogy, perseverance in holiness is not a desirable extra in the Christian life, but an indispensable necessity to final salvation. Verse fourteen sums it up perfectly: '...without holiness no one will see the Lord.' But just as there is no *obtaining* without *persevering*, so there is no *persevering* without *trusting*. Here in verses one and two the writer marries them together: (and those whom God has joined, 'let no man put asunder!') Yes, we do need to 'throw off everything that hinders, and the sin that so easily entangles', but the writer does not stop there. He goes on, and adds this: 'Let us fix our eyes on Jesus.' This too is absolutely essential.

The double cure

To believe you are saved, and therefore safe, but are not endeavouring by the grace of God to have done with sin, is a contradiction in terms. This is because the whole purpose for which the Lord Jesus Christ came to die in our place was to save us *from* our sins, not *in* them. The angelic annunciation to Joseph at the first Christmas was, '...you are to give him the name Jesus, because he will save his people from their sins.' (Matt. 1:21). So with Augustus Toplady, the true convert's prayer will always be:

> Be of sin the *double* cure,
> Cleanse me from its guilt *and* power.

This is a great test of where we stand. We cannot have a divided Christ. If we receive him as *Saviour*, we must also receive him as *Lord*, because he is never the one without the other.

Fix our gaze

However, and it is crucial we grasp this principle, that is only one side of the coin. The other side is that the only way in which we can persevere in obedience to the revealed will of God in Scripture, is as we fix our gaze on Jesus.

It becomes obvious now why this other side also needs to be stressed. As with many of these Hebrews, no doubt some of us are cast down and discouraged. There can be a number of reasons for this condition, but almost invariably it comes back to one of two things – or it may well be both of them together.

On the one hand there are the personal trials and disappointments we suffer in this life; while on the other there is the whole state of the world outside, together with the apparent ineffectiveness of the people of God in making any real impact on the situation. And yet, here are people who are already low and dispirited, being warned that it is vital for their eternal life that they 'keep on keeping on'.

If we *only* emphasized the thought of verse one, without taking it in conjunction with verse two, it would be calculated to make such people even more depressed! It would be easy to become daunted by what is involved and the standard set: so daunted, in fact, as to cry out, 'Who then *can* be saved?' (Mark 10:26). Many of the Hebrews felt that they were weary and downhearted already, so what possibility did they have of persevering to the end? This may be your own situation! We know that in our own strength we do not possess the necessary endurance and feel sure we will fall away. So what is the answer? It is here in verse two; and what a glorious answer it is! 'Let us fix our eyes on Jesus, the author and perfecter of our faith.' This is the only way.

This is particularly relevant in view of the increase in crime figures and the alarming increase in groups whose aim is anarchy. In Great Britain the politicians periodically attack the Church of England for failing to give a proper moral lead to the nation, while many churchmen respond by criticizing the government of the day for inner-city deprivation, and for not pouring enough funds into social and welfare aid.

But both sides are wrong because both have entirely missed the point. All sides say they want to see an improvement in moral standards. However, in the same way that there is no perseverance in holiness without a steadfast faith in the Lord

Jesus, so too there will be no return to moral basics until there is a return to the gospel. As one writer has put it: 'Morality has become an orphan, and it has become an orphan because its father, doctrinal belief, has been well-nigh killed off; and that by the professing church herself.' And orphans are weak and vulnerable, are they not?

Look to him

Both the government and the church in Great Britain are struggling to contain the fearful moral landslide that is threatening to engulf our society. But according to the message of the Bible, there will be no *moral* renewal until there is *spiritual* renewal. And a true spiritual renewal will only come as men and women look to our Lord and Saviour, and trust in his redeeming work.

There are still some people who do see the importance of maintaining high moral standards. From a worldly standpoint their personal integrity is unquestionable. They believe in self-discipline, and seek to leave the world a better place than they found it: maybe you are one of them? All credit to you if you are. But no matter how hard you try, and whatever effort is put in, by your own strength and ability you will never be able to complete the race that is marked out in the Bible. Indeed, you are not in the race at all! You have not even begun. The great question facing every one of us is, 'How can I get to heaven, and enter into eternal life?' The Bible tells us there is only *one* way.

> Turn your eyes upon Jesus,
> Look full in his wonderful face.
> *Mrs. H.H. Lemmel*

He alone

Jesus alone can forgive us from the guilt of sin, and he alone can give us power to lay aside sin and resist temptation. Furthermore, 'when all things seem against us, to drive us to despair'[1], he alone can enable us to persevere, and yet do so rejoicing. He alone can enable us to smile in adversity. Our Lord himself said, 'If anyone would come after me, he must deny himself and take up his cross daily *and follow me.*' (Luke 9:23). The Christian life is the most wonderful life there is, but it is also the most demanding. Who am I to live such a life, weak and feeble sinner that I am? There is only one way. In Paul's letter to the Philippians we read: 'I can do everything through him who gives me strength.' (4:13). Have you seen it? The person who has says with the hymnist:

> I need Thee every hour,
> Stay Thou nearby.
> *A.S. Hawkes*

Let us then turn our gaze on him.

JESUS – THE SOLE OBJECT OF FAITH

The word rendered in the New International Version (NIV) as 'fix' has a fuller meaning in the original Greek. In fact, it is the only occurrence of this term in the entire New Testament. The King James or Authorized Version (KJV/AV) translates it as 'looking unto Jesus', but that is inadequate because it is too weak. The only version that really captures the meaning here seems to be Weymouth's Translation, which renders it as 'Looking *off* (or away) unto Jesus.' The significance of that should be obvious. It means that we must not only keep our eyes – our spiritual gaze – on Jesus; 'fixing' it on him, as the NIV has it, but to do so taking our eyes off everyone and everything else. It means that we must fix our gaze on him, and on him *alone*, as the object of faith. The teaching here is that saving faith is never, nor can be, divided in its object. The Christian does not trust in Moses and Jesus, and he does not trust in Mohammed and Jesus.

We rest our faith in him *alone*,
Who died for our transgressions to atone.

We are to do so to the exclusion of everyone else, without exception. In the words of the Apostle Paul: 'Other foundation can no man lay than that is laid, which is Jesus Christ' (1 Cor. 3:11 KJV).

On Christ the solid Rock I stand;
All other ground is sinking sand.
E. Mote

Can you say that? In order to run this race successfully, the Christian has to 'press toward the mark', but always keeping his eye on the one who is waiting for him there at the finish; ready to reward him with 'the prize of the high calling of God.'

Look away

This is the only way to persevere in the Christian life. You must look away from others, away from yourself and your own fancied righteousness, and even away from all the trials and vicissitudes of life, and look *only* to him, and his righteousness. We are not to make even the cross our object of faith, but only him who *was* dead, but is alive for evermore. We are not enjoined to look *backwards* to an *event*, but rather to look *upwards* to a *person*, who is seated on the throne of the universe. What are we told here about him?

JESUS — THE PERFECT EXPRESSION OF FAITH

We need to note that 'our' is not in the original, which is why the KJV puts it in italics, 'the author and perfecter of *our* faith.' Really, it should not be in the text at all, because it gives a misleading impression. The Lord is being spoken of here not so much as the author and perfecter of *our* faith – though that is true – but as the author and perfecter of faith *as such*. When we also realize that the term *author* is again a rather unfortunate rendering of the original, and that it should be *pioneer*, it puts a completely different slant on the whole passage. Bearing all that in mind, we need to consider the two great words in turn.

The Pioneer

To start with, our Lord is set forth as the *pioneer* of faith, and in a sense that is self-explanatory. For instance, those who remember their history will know that the pioneer of steam locomotion in Britain was George Stephenson. He was the man who took the lead in this respect, and went ahead in it. In the same way, the Lord Jesus Christ has led the way in the life of faith. In fact, some expositors have rendered it, 'Looking away unto Jesus, the *file-leader* of faith.' He was the 'trail-blazer' in this particular field of endeavour – the one whose entire life on earth was the very embodiment of trust in God as his heavenly Father, as we see so perfectly in the gospel record. As Philip Hughes says in his commentary on Hebrews: 'In looking to Jesus, then, we are looking to him who is the supreme exponent of faith, the one who, beyond all others, not only set out on the course of faith, but pursued it without wavering to the end.'[2] He never faltered, never gave up. And as the pioneer, he enables us to follow in his steps.

> Our glorious Leader claims our praise
> For His own pattern given;
> While the long cloud of witnesses
> Show the same path to heaven.
> *Isaac Watts*

The perfecter

However, the Lord is not only described as the *pioneer* of faith, but as the *perfecter* of faith; not *finisher*, as in the KJV. In line with our understanding of the first term, *pioneer*, this does not mean that Jesus completes, or perfects *our* faith, (though needless to say, he does). It means rather that he is the perfecter of faith as such, so that in him, we see faith perfectly expressed. To put it another way, he is the supreme and final model of faith in practice – he is way ahead of the rest of the field in this respect – towering above everyone else, Old Testament and New Testament saints alike. Of course, it is here that all the human analogies break down. George Stephenson was certainly the pioneer in the matter of steam locomotion, as Jesus was the pioneer of faith. But, unlike Stephenson, nothing that our Lord did can be improved on. Stephenson's work was superseded by later giants of the steam age – Churchward, Gresley and others – but that was not the case with the Lord Jesus Christ.

In him, we see faith at its zenith and acme; absolutely perfect. Here he stands alone. He is, if you like, 'the man of faith' *par excellence*. In the words of Thomas Goodwin, the Puritan, 'Jesus Christ was the greatest and best believer that ever lived.'

> In Thee, most perfectly expressed,
> The Father's glories shine.
> *Josiah Conder*

Read the four gospels, and it is clear that from start to finish his whole course was marked out and characterized by complete faith in God, whatever the opposition, trials and suffering he had to endure. 'Hallelujah, what a Saviour!' – and just the kind of Saviour we need.

JESUS – THE SUPREME EXAMPLE OF FAITH

It is because Jesus is the perfect expression of faith, that as our Great High Priest he is uniquely qualified to not only *supply*, but to *sustain* the faith of his tried and tempted followers. So we must look to him accordingly, he who 'endured the cross, scorning

its shame.' What an amazing faith he had! *We* have the help
and encouragement of friends in time of need and we thank
God for them. But at those times of greatest suffering and testing for *him*, our Lord stood utterly alone. Even his closest disciples
all forsook him and fled. His was a faith that endured even
Gethsemane and the cross, with its agony and shame. 'He trod
the winepress alone!'

The only answer

This has tremendous implications for us all. As with the readers
of this letter, we too might be going through a difficult and trying time. It may be something that no one else knows of – 'the
heart knoweth its own bitterness' – and we are weary and
discouraged, tempted to give in and give up. The devil whispers
that God does not care, or else why does he allow it? What is
the answer? It is both simple and yet profound. We are to fix our
eyes anew on Jesus, and look away to him! Think of what he
endured! With Isaac Watts begin anew to 'survey the wondrous
cross'. And yet Christ was the Son of God! Why did he do it?
Because he took the long view, 'the joy set before him'!

We can fitly close this chapter with an illustration from Greek
mythology. The story tells how a certain king offered his daughter
Atalanta's hand in marriage to anyone who could outrun her.
But no one could, although many tried. And if you tried and
failed, you would lose your head! Then one day a young man
named Milanion entered. The race had not gone far when again
it seemed that he too was going to lose. But unlike the others,
Milanion had prepared for this eventuality. He had three golden
apples, and as Atalanta began to outstrip him, he rolled one
into her path. Thinking she could easily catch up again, she
stopped to pick it up, and soon made up lost ground. So Milanion
used the second apple, but again she caught up and began to
overtake him. Finally, he used his last apple, but this time Atalanta
had overestimated the time she had left and Milanion reached
the tape first.

That is a helpful picture of what happens to so many who make a Christian profession. They start well, or so it seems. But then the world, the flesh, and the devil start rolling the golden balls in front of them; the things 'that hinder and the sin that so easily entangles' begin to distract them. There is only one remedy, but thank God it is a sovereign one. Look away from it all, even from the trials and anxieties.

Look ever to Jesus,
He will carry you through.
H.R. Palmer

3 | the Christian's fainting fits

Consider him who endured such opposition from sinful men, so that you will not grow weary and lose heart. In your struggle against sin, you have not yet resisted to the point of shedding your blood.'

Hebrews 12:3-4

Many of the people to whom the author was writing had become acutely discouraged in the Christian life. This was largely due to the sufferings they were experiencing, particularly the antagonism and even persecution they were enduring from their unbelieving compatriots, the Jews. As a result some of them were back casting wistful eyes to the old life of Judaism in which they had been reared. They simply could not understand why God was permitting these trials. After all, if Jesus really was the promised Messiah, then why were all these terrible things happening to them? It just did not make sense.

Then, as invariably happens, the devil came in with his insinuations and innuendos, suggesting that they had made a terrible mistake and should never have left Judaism in the first place. They should return to Moses where they belonged.

But, according to the writer of this wonderful letter, there is nothing as fraught with spiritual danger as that kind of attitude. It is not difficult to see why. The Lord Jesus Christ, as the mediator of the New Covenant, is God's last and final word to mankind. In him the process of divine revelation is brought to its consummation, and therefore to go back from Jesus to

Moses is in reality to go back to perdition. Moses and the law, vital though it is for the purposes for which God gave it, can never atone for sin. Only Jesus Christ can do that; and the great message of the New Testament is that he *has* done that, once and for all.

Preservation and perseverance

The writer to the Hebrews is alarmed lest his readers had not fully grasped the full significance of what he had said. So out of a deep pastoral concern, he urges them not to even think about going back, but rather to keep going through every situation, however difficult it may be. Notice how he does so in the second half of verse one, where he exhorts them to 'run with perseverance the race' that is marked out for them. There we have one of the great classic New Testament statements of the doctrine of perseverance. And no better illustration could be used than the analogy of running a race. It 'reminds us very forcefully,' writes Professor John Murray, 'that only those who persevere to the end are truly saints. We do not attain to the prize of the high calling of God in Christ Jesus automatically.'[1] If we drop out of the race, we will be lost.

Maybe some are puzzled at this point, even confused. After all, does the Bible not teach that a true Christian *cannot* fall away and be finally lost? The Lord himself says about his followers, 'I give them eternal life, and they shall never perish; no-one can snatch them out of my hand' (John 10:28). Why then are these Hebrews warned so solemnly about the peril of falling away? It seems contradictory. What is the explanation?

It is this: that both propositions are true. God does preserve his people, but *his* preserving is always evidenced by *our* persevering. Failure to persevere is not proof that believers can fall away. All it proves is that 'it is possible to give all the outward signs of faith in Christ...and then lose all interest and become indifferent.'[2] It indicates that such were not genuine believers in the first place, and had never been truly born again. The reason why believers are given such fearful warnings in Scripture has been well explained by C.H. Spurgeon in a sermon preached on final perseverance in 1856. 'God,' he says, 'preserves his children from falling away; but he keeps them by the use of means; and one of these is, the terrors of the law, showing them what would happen if they were to fall away…It is calculated to excite fear; and this holy fear keeps the Christian from falling.'[3]

Positive encouragement

However, warning us of the awful consequences of going back is only *one* of the means by which we are kept. That is the negative side of the equation, and although not to be despised, there is a higher and greater motivation to persevere. That comes out in the very positive encouragements we are given. Ultimately, there is only one way whereby anyone can press on in the Christian life in the route that Scripture has 'marked out for us'. It is by fixing our gaze on Jesus, our great High Priest, who has trod the pilgrim way before us. It is by *faith* as well as patient *perseverance* that we will inherit the promises, (chapter 6:12). But that is not all. Trial is such a real difficulty in spiritual experience, and is such a common problem, that the writer to the Hebrews goes into it in greater detail. He is concerned to comfort and encourage all who are suffering as Christians; whatever forms that suffering may take. We need to follow him as he does so.

A SERIOUS CONDITION

It is here at the end of the third verse, where he draws attention to the danger of *growing weary* and *losing heart*. In passing, it is very interesting, and even significant, that the writer to the Hebrews does not actually say that his readers *were in* that state. There is not much doubt that some – maybe many – of them were, but he does not say that in so many words. All he does is to explain to them how to avoid getting into such a pitfall and by implication how to extricate themselves if they do. There is a saying; 'prevention is better than cure', and what he prescribes for us here is a spiritual prophylactic; preventative medicine for the ailments of the soul.

Pastoral sensitivity

In doing so, we are given a wonderful piece of true Biblical psychology, which highlights the great pastoral concern and sensitivity that the author shows for his readers. He does not want to make them feel worse than they do already – for then they will only become more dispirited. Therefore he does not repeatedly tell them what a dreadful condition they are in. That approach rarely, if ever, improves the situation. He is more tactful than that, and makes his point by telling them how to prevent ever getting into this depressive state. He uses the same positive approach elsewhere in this letter.

To give just one illustration, he puts it like this in chapter six, verse nine: 'Even though we speak like this, dear friends, we are confident of better things in your case – things that accompany salvation.' In the preceding verses, he had spoken very severely of the danger of apostasy, and in so doing had made it clear that such a condition was irremediable. 'It is impossible,' he says, if you fall away, 'to be brought back to repentance.' But in case that led to further doubt and discouragement, he adds this note of confidence and optimism.

The principle here is a vital one in our dealings with one another. It is exactly the same at the natural level. Any parent worthy of the name, will know that if they want their child to be successful in anything – be it sports or schoolwork – they do not say, 'You will never do well in that; you are hopeless.' What you do rather is encourage, and give the child all the motivation and incentive you can.

Cast down

However the word translated as 'weary' (in both the NIV and

the KJV), is too weak a rendering. It has a much stronger connotation in the original. Literally, it means to be *exhausted*; so this contestant is not just a bit tired. Rather, he is so weary as to be at the point of dropping out of the race altogether. Some of these Hebrews were so cast down as the result of the trials they were going through, that they had lost all heart for persevering in the Christian life, and were in danger of giving up altogether, as verse twelve makes clear. Here are believing people, for whom the experience of suffering and persecution on the one hand, together with the constant problem of dealing with the entanglements of sin on the other, have combined to produce a spiritual weariness they found hard to throw off. Indeed, the person who falls into this condition becomes so depressed, and even hopeless, that they feel they cannot go a step further. It is all too much for them.

How well the Scripture knows us! Probably everyone who is reading these lines has felt like this at some time or another.

It is important to realize that these believers had not gone astray in any obvious sense, either doctrinally or morally. The author of Hebrews does not have to rebuke them either for heresy (as in the case of the Galatians), or immorality (as with the Corinthians). Here, he is not concerned with either of those issues, because they are not the main problem.

Satan's subtlety

But that is what makes this situation so subtle. Sometimes believers do find themselves in trouble because they have gone astray theologically, or they have backslidden and fallen into sin, either secretly or publicly. In either case, the problem is a fairly straightforward one, in that the root cause of the difficulty is more obvious and can be dealt with accordingly. But Satan is nothing if not devious, and if he cannot lead a person astray either doctrinally or morally, then he will try a different tack. What we see in these Hebrew believers is a case in point. They had not gone astray in any outward sense, and it is not easy to see what has gone wrong. They are keeping to the course marked out for them, and appear to be going in the right direction.

The trouble is that their progress, if one can call it such, has been reduced to a shuffle. As verse twelve puts it so descriptively, they had 'feeble arms and weak knees'. They looked very sorry for themselves – the very antithesis of what the Christian is meant to be. It is a condition we recognize in others but do we see it in ourselves? Hebrews chapter six, verse twelve, warns us against allowing such laziness to develop.

Comfortable routine

This is a very common problem in the Christian life. There is that initial experience in which everything is new and exciting; but then we can enter a stage of stagnation. Because we think we know it all we are no longer thrilled by fresh discoveries as we were at the outset. Our very familiarity with spiritual issues becomes a stumbling block to further progress. The consequence with so many people is that they settle down into a comfortable routine in which they are going through the motions, but there appears to be no development and growth. What happens then so frequently, is that when problems and trials begin to multiply, they are in real trouble. They are no longer able to surmount these hurdles by the momentum of that initial enthusiasm, and down they go! This is a serious condition, because if it is not checked, it is the first step on the downward path that leads to complete shipwreck of soul.

THE SPIRITUAL CAUSE OF THIS CONDITION

We need to realize that it does have a *spiritual* cause, even though we try to persuade ourselves otherwise. When we grow weary, fainthearted, or start to lag behind in the Christian race, what happens so often is that, in order to justify ourselves, we look around for something or someone on whom to pin the blame. But, as Shakespeare saw so clearly, 'the fault, dear Brutus, lies not in our stars, but in *ourselves…*'

Speak to any person who has gone back from an initial Christian profession and you will find that, almost without exception, they will blame everyone and everything but themselves. This is the kind of situation I have in mind: 'Oh yes, I used to believe in God and go to church, but I have had a lot of trouble in my life, and I cannot seem to find the time these days.' Or it may be that a loved one became ill, and their prayers for healing were not answered. The result is that their faith in a God of love can be irreparably shaken.

True psychology

What then is the underlying cause of this condition? The writer to the Hebrews clearly tells us, and in so doing, we have a further example of the wonderful spiritual insight he had, by the grace of God. Here, we have the true psychology, a masterly analysis of this whole spiritual condition.

This is how he puts it: 'so that you will not grow weary and lose heart.' Both the NIV and the KJV read as if weariness and losing heart are just two different ways of referring to what is essentially the same thing. But, according to the commentators, that is not so. A better rendering would be this: 'so that losing heart, you grow weary.' One of the best translations at this point is that of the New English Bible: 'Think of him who submitted to such opposition from sinners: that will help you not to lose heart and grow faint.'

Universal principle

In other words, growing faint, or weary, is the *consequence* and *result* of losing heart. Once that is realized, it throws a flood of light on this condition. In fact, it highlights what is a universal principle, which is also true at the physical level. We know if the heart is weak then that will affect the whole body and can cause extreme tiredness and even complete exhaustion. It is no use the sufferer dosing himself with some form of pep pill; that may give a temporary 'lift', but only for a while, and the condition will soon return in an even worse form.

What the man needs is a proper diagnosis of the *cause* of his condition, rather than just treating the symptoms. This principle is also true in the realm of psychology. To give just one example from the realm of sport, we need go no further than the annual British Inter-Varsity boat race between Oxford and Cambridge. In the year 2000 Oxford won after several years of defeat – and it showed! Both crews had expended roughly the same amount of energy, but after the finishing line was crossed, only those in the Cambridge boat looked weary. In fact they were utterly drained. By contrast, the victorious Oxford crew looked exuberant enough to row the Putney to Mortlake course all over again!

The difference is that one crew had lost and were downhearted, whereas the other had won and were in good heart. Because they were in such good heart, they were not conscious of being weary at all. On the contrary, they felt full of energy. And it was evident! It all comes back to the heart. There is a little rhyming couplet that goes like this:

> Two men looked out from prison bars;
> One saw mud, and the other saw stars.

Their circumstances were identical, but their individual responses could not have been more different. It all depends on the state of heart. One man was gloomy and pessimistic, so he only saw the mud, whereas the other was hopeful and optimistic, and he saw the stars.

The joy of the Lord

What is true at the physical and psychological levels, is equally true in the realm of the Spirit, and in Christian experience. There is a perfect illustration of this in the ministry of Nehemiah. This is what he said to the men engaged in rebuilding the walls of Jerusalem: '...the joy of the LORD is your strength!' (Nehemiah 8:10).

That is the cure to the problem of spiritual weariness; the joy of the Lord in the heart. George Whitefield said on one occasion, 'I am weary *in* the work, but not weary *of* the work', and there is a world of difference between the two. Yes, Whitefield was *physically* weary, not surprisingly in view of his almost Herculean labours, but he was not *spiritually* weary because he had not lost *heart.*

The power of the Spirit

But we need to probe a little deeper because if the cause of spiritual depression and weariness lies in the heart, why do Christians lose heart in the first place? No doubt there are a number of possible explanations for this condition, but the main reason is undoubtedly this: so often, we try to live the Christian life and engage in the work of the Lord in our own energy rather than in the power of the Spirit. We have been trying to do God's work by the exercise of merely human strength, to please ourselves. What we need to ask ourselves is why have we been doing the work at all? What has been the motive? We tend to assume that our motives are pure – but *are* they? The truth is that it is terribly possible to be actively involved in Christian work simply because you are of the type that thrives on activity and organising things. But if we live on our own activities, then sooner or later, when we can no longer do what we used to do – by reason of advancing years and physical infirmity – we will not know what to do with ourselves. Inevitably, we will become depressed, especially when afflictions come.

Dr. Martyn Lloyd-Jones constantly warned pastors and preachers of the danger of living on one's own preaching, rather than on Christ himself. But as surely as we live on *any* activity, rather than on *him*, our blessed Lord and Saviour, so surely will we become weary *of* the work as well as weary *in* it.

THE SCRIPTURAL CURE

To start with, what we must not do is give up, however strong the temptation to do so – because *it is* a temptation. Whatever I may *feel*, whatever the provocation, I must immediately reject the voice that whispers to me that I cannot keep going and therefore the only thing to do is give in. Maybe you are weary and tired, and it is all getting too much. But refuse to listen to the siren song of the tempter. The old hymn says 'Yield *not* to temptation!' Rather, say this to yourself: 'Whatever happens, and however I *feel*, I am going *on!*'

So much for the negative: what we must *not* do. But once we have taken a definite stand on that position, what must we do in a more positive sense? Let me suggest two vital principles at this point:

Realization

The first is the need of *realization*, the realization that other believers have had an infinitely worse time than I have, but *they* did not give up. In chapter ten, verse thirty-three, the author refers to some who were 'publicly exposed to insult and persecution', others who were imprisoned, and still others who had lost their property because of the faith. Here is a great lesson. We thought our problem was the most terrible trial in the world, did we not? No one had suffered as we had!

We look round the church, and there is someone who has been widowed at an early age, another who is seriously disabled – and *they* have not gone back. That puts our problem into a new perspective immediately. The Apostle Paul refers to this in writing to the Corinthians: 'No temptation (or *trial* – it is the same word) has seized you except what is common to man. And God is faithful.' (1 Cor. 10:13). The devil will try to persuade us that *our* trouble is unique. Needless to say that is not true. Some of God's greatest servants have experienced trials and troubles that cause ours to pale into complete insignificance. But they stood fast; in some cases they were even martyred. Just to realize that fact is a great help, but do not stop there. The final cure, the sovereign remedy for this sorry condition, is emphasized yet again at the beginning of verse three. '*Consider* him who endured such opposition from sinful men, so that you will not grow weary and lose heart.'

Consideration

The second thing then is *consideration*. 'Consider him!' Finally, it all comes back to Christ, and what he has done. He left the glory everlasting for our sakes, and he endured it all – the vilification and all that went with it – even to the extent of dying for us and suffering the wrath of God against our sin.

> In my place condemned he stood,
> Sealed my pardon with his blood.
> Hallelujah! What a Saviour!
> *P.P. Bliss*

That is it! You and I have the inestimable privilege of following in his steps. Ask him then to forgive you for ever moaning and feeling sorry for yourself, and continue to consider him, in all the glory of his person, and the perfection of his finished work.

4 | consider him!

'Let us fix our eyes on Jesus…who for the joy set before him endured the cross, scorning its shame, and sat down at the right hand of the throne of God. Consider him who endured such opposition from sinful men…'

Hebrews 12:2-3

What stands out on the very surface of this great letter is the author's deep concern – not to say anxiety – about the people to whom he was writing. The reason for his disquiet is not difficult to discern for, as we established at the opening of the previous chapter, these Hebrew Christians could not understand how their belief on the promised Messiah had not removed the trials and problems from their lives.

Looking back

According to the writer to the Hebrews, there is nothing quite as perilous to the soul as wondering if you have 'done the right thing' by becoming a Christian. Jesus Christ is God's last and final word to this world. The whole of divine revelation meets in him, and comes to full fruition in him. Therefore to go back from him is to go back from God!

Because of the writer's solicitude for his readers, his words are to encourage them, and to explain the meaning and purpose of these troubles: the rationale in the dealings of God with his children. However, he also does warn them; and chapters six and ten contain some of the most solemn warnings in the entire Bible.

But, as we see from the postscript in chapter thirteen, verse twenty-two, the predominant note throughout the letter is one of encouragement: 'Brothers, I urge you to bear with my word of *encouragement*' – or that is how it should read. Both the NIV and the KJV translate it as *exhortation*, but the experts tell us that the word is softer and gentler in the original. Perhaps the best rendering is that of the Good News Bible: 'I beg you brothers, listen patiently to this message of encouragement.' And encouragement was what these early believers needed, as we all do, especially during times of trial. The writer realized they were weary and had lost heart, so he administers what he knew was the sovereign remedy for that condition.

Reflection

It is to 'Consider *him*', and to keep our gaze on him, our Lord and Saviour. Ultimately, this is the only way to deal with the gloomy, depressed state of mind. The solution of this common problem is not by refusing to think, as some folk seem to imagine, but by actually stirring ourselves up to think more! How well the Scripture knows us! Most of our troubles in the Christian life are caused by a failure to think. This is where the situation needs to be addressed, hence the urgent exhortation here to *consider* the Lord Jesus Christ. Consideration implies *thought* – it involves reflection and study, and with the subject-matter being this wonderful person, we should not begrudge the effort this requires.

In seeking to help people in their trials, the answer is not just 'pray about it'. Prayer and consideration are not incompatible. Rather, they go together like twins. But the point needs to be made, because there are some well-meaning Christians who, when they are offering counsel to someone who is passing through deep waters, have a standard piece of advice: 'pray about it'! Of course we should pray about everything, and in every situation. But simply to say 'pray about it' can be very glib and simplistic. It is not the New Testament method of dealing with trial and affliction, which never makes prayer a *substitute* for thought.

State of panic

If all we were supposed to do in time of trouble was to pray about it, a great deal of pastoral instruction in these letters need never have been written. Prayer can be a mechanism to *avoid* thinking, and can be uttered more in a state of panic than of faith. That is how the unbeliever reacts to trouble. In his blind fear he will blurt out a prayer for help, but with no real idea of to whom he is praying.

I have vivid memories of one of the most terrible nights of the blitz during the Second World War. I was about seven at the time and, along with my mother and a number of neighbours, I spent the night in an Air Raid shelter, while the Luftwaffe were raining bombs and incendiaries on London. I shall never forget how some of those people, desperately frightened, who never had any time for God before (or after, to my knowledge), began to pray out aloud in their fear. No shyness or embarrassment then about calling on God in prayer! But was it believing prayer? Surely true prayer is not panic-stricken, as if turning to God as a last resort. What an insult to God to use him in this way.

Although we should always 'pray continually' (1 Thess. 5:17), our praying should never be at the *expense* of thought, or an excuse for not thinking. The problem with these Hebrews lay in their understanding, their failure to keep in mind the teaching they had received and apply it to their own situation. So the writer does not just exhort them to pray, he reminds them of the doctrine, and in particular the doctrine of Christ. *Consider him!* This means much more than give him a passing glance. To *consider* him means that you focus your thoughts on him, you concentrate upon his person and the truth concerning him. This involves the activity of the mind.

The word 'consider' is a special and interesting term. It really means, 'consider by way of comparison', or 'by way of analogy'. Indeed, our English word 'analogy' comes from the Greek rendered as 'consider'. So it means when, because of our tribulations we are tempted to give up, we consider how greatly the Lord suffered by comparison with the relatively minor troubles that we encounter.

However, the writer to the Hebrews does not exhort us to consider the Saviour and then hurry on to the next point. He goes into details, and we must follow him as he does so.

A DESCRIPTION OF HIS SUFFERINGS

Notice how it is put in verse two: 'Let us fix our eyes on Jesus, who *endured the cross, scorning its shame.*' Only a few words but what a wealth of meaning they contain! Think for a moment of the *physical* sufferings involved. He endured the *cross*, which Cicero, the famous Roman senator, described as 'that most brutal and horrifying torture'. There is a very real sense in which death by crucifixion is the most cruel and agonising way to die that was ever invented. In the world of that day, any death was considered preferable to death by crucifixion. So come with me in spirit to Calvary – what do we see?

The cross

Jesus had already had his back cut to ribbons by the flogging he received in Pilate's Hall – so severe a punishment that many men did not survive it. But now the cross itself is to follow. The rough timber is thrown on the ground, and Jesus is flung on it on his back. Iron spikes are then hammered through his hands and feet, pinning him to the wood in agonising pain. Worse is to come, for as that cross is raised and thrust into its socket, the victim's joints would be dislocated by that fearful, shuddering jerk. But even that is not all because all the authorities are agreed that the most terrible aspects of crucifixion are the raging thirst and the excruciating cramps which cannot be relieved.

The shame

Consider him! Think of him as he hung there on that Roman gibbet, in the anguish and the unimaginable torment of it all. But do not allow your thought process to stop there because our greatest need is to realize that our Lord's bodily sufferings, horrific as they undoubtedly were, are as nothing compared to the indescribable sufferings of soul he endured. The writer to the Hebrews speaks of the *shame* involved, and even at the human level nothing more disgraceful and ignominious could happen to any man than to suffer public execution in that form. It was a fate reserved for the lowest and most degraded of criminals and social outcasts. A death so degrading that no Roman citizen could be subjected to it; there was no lower depth of indignity and humiliation.

In varying ways, our Lord had endured opposition from sinful men throughout his earthly life and ministry. But that malign and implacable hostility reached its climax on the cross, where he was made the innocent butt of the world's derision and contempt. Listen to them as they scoff and jeer, 'He saved others, himself he cannot save!' The pelting scorn and ridicule he endured is almost too awful to contemplate, and yet we are urged to do so. To be mocked by evil men is a fearful trial, but it was the *shame* of the cross that caused him such an intensity of suffering. Other men have suffered the physical agony of crucifixion, and endured the scoffing of the crowd who have come to gape on the spectacle. But our Lord alone has borne the shame of being punished for human sin in all its depravity and foulness. There on the cross the Lord Jesus Christ was '*made sin for us, who knew no sin*' (2 Cor. 5:21 KJV).

> Bearing shame and scoffing rude,
> In my place condemned he stood.
> *P.P. Bliss*

Forsaken

There, Christ was counted as guilty in our place. In him, the full demands of the holy law of God were met, both actively and passively. On Calvary's hill, God the Father spared him nothing that was due as punishment for our sin. We will never know his degree of suffering – to be separated from all sense of the love and comfort of his Father, whose fellowship he delighted in – is far beyond even the redeemed comprehension. All he was conscious of was the *wrath* of God. That awful cry of dereliction wrung from his lips and from his heart gives us a hint, but only a hint: 'My God, my God, why have you forsaken me?' He was 'despised and rejected by men', but terrible thought though it is, he was despised and rejected by God too! Mrs. C.F. Alexander was right when she penned:

> We may not know, we cannot tell
> What pains he had to bear.

But we can *consider* it – and we can add this – we who trust in his redeeming blood:

> But we believe it was for us
> He hung and suffered there.

OUR LORD'S REACTION

This is graphically described for us in just two words. In the first place, he *endured* the cross. The word really means '*patiently endured*' and in a context that is emphasizing the vital necessity of perseverance, we are pointed to the tremendous example that was set us. It means that he went right through with it to the bitter end. Recall how he prayed in the Garden of Gethsemane, 'My Father, if it is possible, may this cup be taken from me...' (Matt. 26:39). Jesus was asking his Father if there was another way; if he could be spared from his Father's wrath and the hiding of his face. But he added '...Yet not as I will, but as you will.'

And it *was* God's will that he should drink that cup; drink it to its last bitter dregs. 'Yet it was the Lord's will to crush him, and cause him to suffer…' (Isa. 53:10). So he gladly acquiesced. he '…became obedient to death – even death on a cross!' (Phil. 2:8).

Clearly, *endurance* here means much more than the tight-lipped stoicism that merely grits its teeth in the face of adversity, and carries on to the bitter end. Rather, it could be said of him: 'I delight to do thy will, O my God…' (Psalm 40:8 KJV). Jesus was never just submissive. Still less was he grudgingly obeying because he *had* to and not because he *wanted* to. On the contrary, he obeyed the will of God cheerfully, from the heart, even though it broke his heart to do so. And in all that he never wavered or faltered; no, not for a second. From the very outset, he had set his face steadfastly to go to Jerusalem. There was no turning back. He *endured* the cross. Consider it, and consider it well!

But he not only '*endured*' the cross. We are told secondly, that in so doing, he was '*scorning* its shame.' When you *scorn* something, you belittle or despise it. You consider it as beneath serious notice, unworthy of serious attention. Now the amazing thing before us is that this is precisely how the Lord Jesus Christ viewed the shame and disgrace that were his lot. All the reproach and obloquy that was heaped upon him he utterly disregarded. He never allowed it for a moment to deflect him from the course he had set himself.

Object of ridicule

It does not mean he never *felt* the shame. He did, and in a way that we will never know. It cut deep into him. But – and this is the thrust here – it never moved him by so much as a hairs-breadth from his objective. We know that there is nothing in life from which we so much tend to shrink as shame. History records many great men for whom death was preferable. To be exposed to the utter contempt of one's peers, to be the object of ridicule and the jeer, can indeed be a 'fate worse than death', an unbearable torture for some. Consequently they have taken their own lives rather than suffer it. There are some people who say, 'I care for nobody and nobody cares for me.' To such folk it is a matter of complete indifference what people think of them, or so they say! But for the Lord this was an especially bitter cup, and we will examine this further.

Jesus crucified for me

Our Lord was so sensitive to the needs of others, so concerned for their eternal welfare, that when his love is treated with such utter contempt it must have been like a dagger-thrust. It added sorrow upon sorrow to his already burdened heart. To come 'to his own', and yet his own to 'receive him not'; to be spat on and then crucified by those he came to save; that was torture indeed! But he never let it deter him. He *scorned* the shame as if it were nothing: a mere triviality. What a wonder it all is! William Walsham How expressed it like this in a hymn:

> I sometimes think about the cross,
> And shut my eyes, and try to see
> The cruel nails, and crown of thorns,
> And Jesus crucified for me.

And yet, the most vivid imagination, the most sanctified mind, can only begin to appreciate and to understand these 'infinities and immensities', as that very hymn goes on to point out:

> But even could I see him die,
> I could but see a little part
> Of that great love which, like a fire,
> Is always burning in his heart.

All we can do is cry out with another hymnist:

O make me understand it,
Help me to take it in,
What it meant to Thee, the Holy One,
To bear away my sin.

K.A.M. Kelly

THE LORD'S MOTIVATION

We find this in verse two: '...who for the joy set before him endured the cross, scorning its shame, and sat down at the right hand of the throne of God.' These words are very significant. There are some Christians who no doubt consider themselves to be very spiritual in saying that they do not serve God in order to gain a reward – because that is an unworthy, selfish motive. But they are claiming higher motives than our blessed Lord himself! The incentive of gaining heaven, and avoiding hell, is a perfectly valid and Scriptural motivation. It is not the *only* motive, but it is a powerful one, and it is an acceptable motive to God that should never be underestimated.

Glorious prospect

What was that joy to which the Lord looked forward, and which enabled him to 'keep on keeping on', even to the death of the cross? It was the joy of saving his people with an eternal salvation! And it was the joy of hearing the Father's 'Well done!' That is why the terrible cry of dereliction was followed by an even louder cry of triumph. 'It is finished!' It was a shout of victory, because nothing else remained to be done. There, in the Garden of Gethsemane, in all the agony and bloody sweat, it was the joy set before him that saw him through. As he staggered up Golgotha, and hung there as a spectacle, it was the reward to come that filled his vision.

This was all prophesied many centuries earlier by Isaiah: 'He shall see of the travail of his soul, and shall be satisfied...' (Isaiah 53:11 KJV). Satisfied because of bringing his many brethren to glory!

All along our Lord had this great objective firmly in view. This was the glorious prospect that sustained him and urged him on: the delightful anticipation of what was to come. This was the joy for which he so willingly became man; the joy for which he bore the antagonism of sinners and for which he was ready even to be 'made sin'. But he did it. He won through, conquering all his enemies, and ours, and completed the work. He then 'sat down at the right hand of the throne of God'. We sit down when our work for the day is completed, something we look forward to. So it was with him.

> All his work is ended,
> Joyfully we sing;
> Jesus hath ascended!
> Glory to our King!
> F.R. Havergal

No one understands

The personal significance of all this is surely obvious. Is this Christian race becoming too arduous? Are you tempted to drop out? What is the answer? Here it is, so simple and yet at the same time so profound. *Consider him!* Maybe our trials are such that we find this hard to reconcile with the Gospel. The *providence* of God seems to be at cross-purposes with the *promises* of God. That is a clear indication that we have not really grasped the meaning of the Gospel. This is the Gospel. 'Consider him who *endured...*' If *he* suffered, why should it come as a great surprise that *we*, who are called to follow in his steps, are suffering? So often we commiserate with ourselves, and tell ourselves, that no one has to go through what we are going through, and no one understands. The trouble with that is there is too much of *self* in it. There is only one way to get rid of self: it is to become so absorbed in someone else that self fades into the background. Here we are shown how the Spirit makes that possible.

The wondrous cross

Consider him! Are you doing so? Are you reminding yourself of this amazing love of Christ, who in spite of our sin and failure, endured the cross and its shame? 'Ah,' we say, 'the same old problems week after week.' No wonder we become weary in the Christian life if that is our attitude. To regard this wonderful life as a dreary task is an insult to God, and to his dear Son. True, the sheer unremitting grind of 'the daily round, the common task' sometimes leads us to think in that way. But there is a remedy! *Consider him!* Think of him who laid aside the glory everlasting and was born as a babe for us. Above all, survey the wondrous cross 'on which the Prince of Glory died'. And keep on considering until your consideration is turned into 'wonder, love, and praise'.

> What language shall I borrow
> To thank Thee, dearest Friend,
> For this Thy dying sorrow,
> Thy pity without end?
> O make me Thine for ever;
> And should I fainting be,
> Lord, let me never, never
> Outlive my love to Thee!
> *Paul Gerhardt*

| # spiritual amnesia

And you have forgotten that word of encouragement that addresses you as sons: "My son, do not make light of the Lord's discipline, and do not lose heart when he rebukes you, because the Lord disciplines those he loves, and he punishes everyone he accepts as a son"'

Hebrews 12:5-6

As we have seen, some of these Hebrew believers were tempted to go back from their faith in Jesus as the promised Messiah, and revert to the Old Testament pattern of life they knew in Judaism. There were a number of reasons why these people had got into such a sorry state. But chiefly, it seems, it was because of the persecution they were suffering as a consequence of their new-found allegiance to this wonderful person, Jesus Christ the Son of God.

However, such a course of action would put their souls in peril and jeopardize their whole eternal future. As the Lord Jesus Christ is God's last and final word to the people, any form of retrogression from him is to court disaster and must inevitably lead to destruction.

Chastisement

Because of the writer's deep concern for his readers, he exhorts and encourages them to 'keep on keeping on' in the Christian life. Here, we are introduced to this vital teaching on chastisement, which is so pervasive in the pages of Holy Scripture – both Old and New Testaments alike. It used to be a common practice for Christians to do a spiritual audit at the commencement of each new year, and examine their lives to see exactly how they were doing.

And yet, as we conduct any period of self-examination, it seems that most of our problems are not caused by adverse circumstances as such, but rather by our failure to respond rightly towards them. Why do we tend to react badly to trials and afflictions? Is not the main reason this, that we forget the Scripture, and lose our grasp on its teaching?

False optimism

That was undoubtedly the underlying cause of the trouble with these Jewish believers, and is why they constantly needed to be reminded of a crucial doctrine of Scripture – one they seem to have lost sight of. This is *the doctrine of sonship* and the discipline that invariably goes with it. What stands out here is the writer's whole method of approach in dealing with these people. He is addressing men and women who had suffered grievously for their faith in Christ. But, unlike the politicians when they are canvassing for votes, he did not try and buoy them up with false hopes. There is no false optimism here – no promises that their trials and tribulations would soon be a thing of the past. Certainly, this man wants to cheer his readers and give them hope, but he does not do that by painting a picture of prosperity and freedom from trouble. Rather, his words are eminently practical and realistic, and yet at the same time we are given the encouragement we need as we go forward into an unknown future.

Source of comfort

You see the immense significance of this passage for us. The writer to the Hebrews was addressing people who lived at a very difficult time in history. So many of our troubles arise from the fact that we tend to think it is only our age that has been exceptionally difficult, and no generation has had to endure troubles such as ours. But when we come to the Bible it always gives us a true and a balanced perspective for, as we look back across the long and chequered story of the people of God, we find that there is nothing unusual in what we have to endure, because it has all happened before.

Uniqueness

That is where the glorious uniqueness of Scripture comes in, because it does not matter in what period of history we live, and whatever is happening to us personally, all our perplexities and difficulties are dealt with. These Hebrew Christians had fallen into this very trap – they could not fathom why *they* were suffering – which is why the quotation from the Old Testament in the second half of verse five is so apposite to their situation. The citation is from Proverbs chapter three, verses eleven and twelve, and by the very fact of quoting from their own Old Testament Scriptures, the writer is demonstrating to these New Testament believers that their troubles were not in any sense unusual or without precedent. Their experience was no different to that of God's children in other ages. Therefore, as the Lord had spoken that word for the encouragement of his suffering saints in the Old dispensation, now the very same word of encouragement is given to New Testament saints.

As we have seen, the writer's great aim is to encourage these Hebrews to press on in the Christian life, and not to draw back, as some were doing. But he does not simply urge them to persevere – he marshals a number of arguments to reinforce his exhortations.

First, he reminds them of the sufferings of our Lord, which were incalculably more severe than anything that *they* had experienced, and yet he went on steadily to the very end. This is the force of the whole appeal in verses two and three – the first consideration to keep in mind and arguably the most powerful. But lest the objection is made that we will never be able to emulate the Lord, or follow his *perfect* example, the writer does not stop there.

Second, he reminds his readers that the sufferings to which they had been exposed were not as severe as those endured by many others: '...you have not yet resisted to the point of shedding your blood' (verse four). No, but others *had!* (Cf. chapter eleven, verse thirty-seven).

But that is still not all, and in verses five and following, he adduces a third consideration, based on the divine purpose of the sufferings these people had undergone.

Ill-founded

It seems that not only Satan, our great adversary, was whispering the lie in their ears that all their troubles were a mark of God's displeasure, and with it a proof that their faith in Jesus as the Messiah was ill-founded – their unbelieving fellow-Jews were saying the same thing. At first this way of thinking does appear to have some force. But the writer shows that these Hebrews were quite wrong and had completely misconstrued the situation. Why? – because they had forgotten the Scriptures. Far from afflictions being a sign that God is *against* you, they are a pointer to the fact that he is *for* you, and is preparing you for glory.

We have already established at the beginning of chapter three that these Jewish believers had misread the situation. They had been brought up to believe that they were God's chosen people; those for whom the Messiah would come. And yet, although the Christ *had* come, and they had believed on him, they had still suffered grievously as a consequence. This was the exact reverse of what they looked for, and it proved a great stumbling-block to their faith. In *their* estimation, they expected a very different lot to what in fact they had experienced. The result was they began to wonder whether Jesus was the promised deliverer after all. Perhaps the best thing for them was to return to the Jewish fold.

It is that misunderstanding which the writer here takes up in verse five, and because it is such a common problem, he deals with it at some length in an extended argument that continues to verse thirteen. But here in verse five, he simply introduces his great theme:

A VITAL NECESSITY

It is the need to keep the Scriptures in the forefront of our minds and in active remembrance. The trouble with so many believers is that in time of trial, they seem to forget the Scriptures. Most of us know this from past experience, that when 'the slings and arrows' of what appears to be 'outrageous fortune' rain down upon us, the immediate instinct is to panic and lose control. Furthermore, when we do let go in that way, we tend to stop thinking spiritually and easily succumb to all kinds of faithless fears. But when we come to the Word of God, the effect is always to steady us by putting the truth before us. It does not say, 'Do not worry, it may never happen', because that does not deal with the problem. Our problem is: suppose it *does* happen, what then? What Scripture does say is that whatever happens makes no difference to our relationship to God, and it cannot touch our soul. It does not matter *what* comes to meet us, it cannot affect our eternal destiny.

Losing touch

The Bible is never out just to soothe and comfort us for the time being. Its message is that there are certain fundamental principles about the life of faith, and if we will only get hold of them, and base our lives upon them, then we can never go seriously astray. The trouble with these Hebrews is that they had lost touch with the relevance of the very Scriptures that in theory they knew so well. So when trouble hit them, they had no answers. Whenever a Christian 'grows weary and loses heart' (as verse three puts it), the cause of the trouble almost invariably stems from this failure to remember the Scriptures, and apply them to present circumstances.

It is amazing that believers can forget such basic passages of Scripture – but it should not surprise us when we do – hence the implicit rebuke. We all have three mighty adversaries ranged against us in this life – the world, the flesh, and the devil. And that infernal trinity is working against us constantly, seeking to divert our attention from these things. We must never lose sight of that, because the Christian life is essentially a *spiritual* battle, not just a question of having a naturally retentive memory. It is absolutely vital that we realize that. We need to draw a sharp distinction between being *aware* of something, and remembering it so that we actually *live* by it and that it controls our lives.

Failing to apply

The fact is, these Hebrews were steeped in the Old Testament – they had been taught these things from the cradle! So when the writer says that they had forgotten this passage from the book of Proverbs, he obviously did not mean that all knowledge of that text had disappeared from their memory-traces. They were not suffering from a medical condition of amnesia (or memory loss), in the *clinical* sense of the word. Their forgetfulness lay in this: when faced by persecution and trials of one kind or another, they were completely failing to *apply* what they knew. If someone had asked these people if they knew Proverbs chapter three, verses eleven and twelve, doubtless they would have acknowledged that they did – just as we would if we were asked if we knew Romans chapter eight, verse twenty-eight. We are all so familiar with that text, are we not? And yet, as we well know, it is perfectly possible to possess that statement in one's *memory*, while it is no help at all in actual *experience*. What goes wrong? It is that we are not applying the teaching of the verse, and its implications, to our own particular situation. Our knowledge, such as it is, is merely theoretical.

This is where preaching comes into its own, because that is what the writer to the Hebrews is engaged in at this juncture. He has written them a letter, but this is much more than cold print. This man is *preaching* what he has to say, and the task of preaching is to arouse the hearers, to stir and awaken them, and to remind them of these matters, because of this terrible tendency in us all to let them slip.

A spiritual issue

However, remembering Scripture in the sense meant here, is much more than memorizing Bible verses off by heart, important as that may be. We cannot remind ourselves of something we do not know and have never learned – so clearly the more of the Bible and its teaching we know by heart, the better. On the other hand, a person could recite the entire book of Proverbs from memory, and yet still react badly to trials.

This is primarily a *spiritual* issue, and is not dependent on a naturally retentive memory. What is needful is that these great truths of Scripture, which we have learnt in the *past*, should exercise a constraining influence upon us in the *present*. The whole secret of success in this matter is not so much a good memory, as a sanctified and obedient life.

Think of those times when, as the result of a powerful message you heard, or an elevating experience of God in prayer, you promised yourself, and God, that you really were going to live on a higher plane in the future. But how easy it is to entirely forget those resolves, and to sink back to the lower level at which we were living before. We did not *mean* to forget, we did not *want* to forget, but we did, and in many ways that is one of the most terrible effects of sin and the Fall upon us.

One can demonstrate that very easily for we tend to forget the things we *want* to remember, and *ought* to remember, while finding it almost impossible to forget the things we *want* to forget, and *ought* to forget. There are some things we would almost give the whole world to forget, are there not? – certain things we have done or said in the heat of the moment; or things that other people have said to us, that rankle and fester in the memory. If only we could erase those episodes from our memory-traces, but we cannot.

The real issue

That is the accursed, perverted element of sin; the thing that makes it so hateful, and so annoying. There is no way it causes our footsteps to stumble more than in this matter of what we remember. So it is never enough to know the Bible passages which teach us that 'the Lord disciplines those he loves.' The real issue is what effect does that truth have on me when I am in the midst of trouble? It is not sufficient to know the passages that teach this vital doctrine; the question is, do I actively remind myself of it in time of trial? Is there instant recall and application? What a crucial matter this is in the life of faith!

A SPIRITUAL PRIORITY

We must keep ourselves constantly exposed to the Word of God. That is an obvious implication because how can I call to mind the relevant Scriptures if I do not read my Bible? We are to pray that the Holy Spirit will help us in this, and bring Scripture to mind as he has promised. But his ministry is not to miraculously reveal texts to us that we have never read, because he has never promised to bless laziness! Rather, 'the soul of the diligent shall be made fat' (Proverbs 13:4 KJV). The function of the Holy Spirit is to stimulate our minds and enable us to recall the things that we already know. In short, head-knowledge of Scripture is essential, even though it is not enough.

Knowing our Bible

This does show up one of the greatest weaknesses among modern Christians: that so many simply do not know their Bibles. Even in my lifetime, and at a time when doctrinally speaking evangelicalism was very weak, it was still a widespread practice in Britain for both adults and children to memorize Scripture. Modern educational theory, in its retreat from the acquisition of 'mere' facts, has influenced the churches far more than they realize. So much so, that this emphasis has almost disappeared from among us. But knowing our Bible and its teaching is absolutely essential. There is only one way to avoid going astray, says the writer to the Hebrews, and that is to view everything in the light of Holy Scripture.

Different complexion

That is the general principle being taught, but here we are shown how that principle applies in a particular case – that of affliction and trouble. Affliction considered merely in itself, and from a human standpoint, only seems to point in one direction – that God is *against* us and is therefore punishing us. But when one considers those afflictions in the light of Scripture, it puts a completely different complexion on everything. Far from being a temptation to *go back*, afflictions for the believer, when they are correctly understood, are incentives to *go on!*

The need to keep ourselves constantly exposed to the Word of God is stressed so frequently and so strongly in Scripture that we could easily take up the rest of the chapter in simply quoting the verses concerned, let alone commenting on them. But here is just a brief selection, taken almost at random, in order to underline the vast importance the Biblical writers attach to this.

Psalm one, verses one and two: 'Blessed is the man who does not walk in the counsel of the wicked or stand in the way of sinners or sit in the seat of mockers. But his delight is in the law of the Lord, and on his law he meditates day and night.'

Psalm one hundred and nineteen – in its entirety is just an extended commentary on this principle, but we can pick out **verse nine** as a classic example: 'How can a young man keep his way pure? By living according to your word.'

John chapter seventeen, verse seventeen, our Lord's High Priestly prayer: 'Sanctify them by the truth; your word is truth.'

Matthew chapter four, verse four: 'Jesus answered, "It is writ-ten: 'Man does not live on bread alone, but on every word that comes from the mouth of God.'"'

Colossians chapter three, verse sixteen: 'Let the word of Christ dwell in you richly as you teach and admonish one another with all wisdom.'

The second letter to Timothy, chapter three, verses sixteen and seventeen: 'All Scripture is God-breathed and is useful for teaching, rebuking, correcting and training in righteousness, so that the man of God may be thoroughly equipped for every good work.'

We have looked at the subject of 'panic prayers' in chapter four' but must remind ourselves here that whenever we find ourselves in a situation of difficulty and of crises, the first thing we must do is to consider it in the light of the relevant Scriptures, praying for guidance and help in order to apply the teaching. We are not just to react to a situation, or give vent to panicky prayers'.

With John Wesley we need to say this: 'I want to know one thing, the way to heaven. God himself has condescended to teach the way: he has written it down in a Book. Oh, give me that Book; at any price give me the Book of God! I have it; here is knowledge enough for me. I sit down alone; only God is here. In his presence I open, I read his Book, for this end, to find the way to heaven.'

When you do, do not read it in the sense of just threading words through your eyes. 'Read, mark, learn, and inwardly digest.' Meditate on it. Work out its implications for you. Soak yourself in it. Marinate your soul in it. As you do so, because this is *the* Book for all seasons, you will find yourself 'a man for all seasons'.

A PERSONAL CERTAINTY

'And you have forgotten that word of *encouragement* that addresses you as *sons*...' The writer is pointing out that because these people had forgotten their Scriptures, and had therefore misread the situation, all they had succeeded in doing was to rob themselves of personal assurance. They had lost their joy, and all because they had (mis)interpreted their circumstances to mean that God was angry with them, and was treating them as enemies.

He tells them that they have missed the point entirely. The word that addresses you is not a word of *judgement*, but a word of *encouragement*. God is not speaking to you as an angry judge to law-breakers, but as a loving, heavenly Father to sons. The fact that he is chastising you, and putting you under discipline, is a *proof* that you are his children! After all, if any *earthly* father worthy of the name exercises discipline in his family, how much more will our *heavenly* Father do so in his!

Spiritual logic

So there is a spiritual logic to these things, which we are expected to work out for ourselves. As the Apostle Paul put it to the Corinthians: 'In understanding be men' (1 Cor. 14:20 KJV). Far from trials having the effect of shaking our faith and spoiling our peace, they are meant to have the opposite effect. They are intended to establish us, and strengthen us, by reminding us that we are in God's hands, and that having begun a good work in us, he will most certainly complete that work. Having delivered up his Son to the cross in our place, he will bring us safely to glory, whatever it takes!

> The work which his goodness began,
> The arm of his strength will complete;
> His promise is Yea and Amen,
> And never was forfeited yet.
> *A.M. Toplady*

6 | sonship

'And you have forgotten that word of encouragement that addresses you as sons: "My son, do not make light of the Lord's discipline, and do not lose heart when he rebukes you, because the Lord disciplines those he loves, and he punishes everyone he accepts as a son."'

Hebrews 12:5-6

It is very important that we keep in mind the circumstances in which this letter was written. Clearly, it was addressed primarily to Jewish converts who were suffering persecution for the faith. In chapter three we looked how these Hebrews were severely distressed by the behaviour of their unbelieving fellow-countrymen but we must not be surprised by this for the Lord himself had predicted, that 'a man's enemies will be the members of his own household.' (Matt. 10:36). They even began to wonder whether in 'looking unto Jesus' for their salvation, they had not made a ghastly mistake for which they were now paying the price. Their reasoning (faulty, as we are seeing), went along the familiar lines that if God was pleased with them why were they suffering? To the eye of sense the argument seems perfectly logical and watertight, as it often does with us.

Does not care

Our situation is not identical to theirs, but in all our lives there are times, when for one reason or another, we go through a period of unusual difficulty and stress; a time when we are subjected to exceptional pressures and strain, and when we may well suffer very great trials of one kind or another. It is then that the temptation comes to us with greatest force; that God does not care, or that the gospel is not living up to its promises. In our weakness the problem can seem unanswerable.

According to the writer to the Hebrews that is to completely misinterpret what is taking place. Far from implying that God is unconcerned about his people's welfare, the hardship and afflictions which these people were undergoing really meant the exact opposite! It showed that he was a true Father to them by treating them as good fathers always will treat their sons; they will discipline and train them. Our heavenly Father knows exactly what we need and what is best for us, so although discipline can seem very hard at times, yet rightly understood it should be a comfort, rather than a discouragement.

Varied methods

However, the reason why we tend to misread these situations is almost invariably this; that we lose touch with our Bibles – hence the quotation in Hebrews from the Book of Proverbs (3:12). As if to say, 'Look, you would never have got into this sorry state if you had remembered your Scriptures!'

Go back over your own experience, especially those times when you were in trouble, and usually you will find that somewhere along the line you had forgotten your Bible and failed to apply the relevant teaching to your own particular circumstances. The inevitable result was a false reading of the situation in which you found yourself, and the almost inevitable discouragement that follows. As Dr. Martyn Lloyd-Jones put it in his well-known book, *Spiritual Depression*: 'A most prolific cause of this condition of spiritual depression is the failure to realize that God uses varied methods in the process of our sanctification.'[1]

One of those methods is chastisement, which can be very painful. It means that our heavenly Father's main concern for us is not so much our *happiness*, but our *holiness*. As the writer puts it in verse fourteen, '...without holiness no one will see the

Lord.' In his great and eternal love for us our Father has determined, indeed guaranteed, to bring us to that glorious goal,
and therefore he will take whatever steps are necessary to get us
there safely.

Of course, the fact that a person has experienced trouble in
life is no proof of being a child of God. In a fallen world like this,
these things come alike to all. The trouble with these Hebrew
Christians was that to them, afflictions seemed to prove they
were not children of God, or if they were, that they had gone
seriously astray.

Glorious purpose

Even if we have not misunderstood trials to that extent, like
foolish children we often feel that God is being unkind to us,
and we are being dealt with very harshly. Yet that whole
syndrome is the result of a failure to grasp the glorious purpose
God has in mind for us. The great problem with these Hebrews,
as with us all at times, was their inability to see the marvel of
their standing in God's household, and the glorious end to which
his fatherly dealings was intended to bring them.

Are you feeling downcast and discouraged, maybe even
resentful at what is happening to you? Finally, there is only one
remedy for that wretched condition; it is to realize that by faith
in the Lord Jesus Christ, you belong to God and are a member
of the family of God. 'High is the rank we now possess', as the
Scottish paraphrase has it, even if 'higher we shall rise.' The
solemn, yet wonderful reality is that discipline is a badge of
sonship, and we constantly need to remind ourselves of that.
This is the main lesson here, which the writer first states in
general in verses five and six, and then further amplifies in verses
seven and following.

A PERSONAL STATUS

The great principle being emphasized throughout this entire
section is that of chastisement. But chastisement, or fatherly

discipline, is only brought in here because it is the inevitable implication of a much bigger and more fundamental doctrine; namely that of of adoption, or sonship. Believers must expect to be disciplined in their Christian lives simply because they are sons of God. Sons by adoption rather than by natural right, but sons nevertheless, with all that goes with this relationship. That is fundamental issue here.

This should not surprise us because like any good human father, God above all is going to be a faithful parent, and ensure that his children grow up to reflect the family honour. He is committed to that, says the writer of Hebrews, and therefore it is what his children can expect.

Verse seven states it in the form of a rhetorical question: '...For what son is not disciplined by his father?' One could be forgiven for wondering if he could say that in the present climate where the norm is for discipline to be capricious, lax, or almost non-existent. However, one cannot miss the great significance that is attached here to the doctrine of sonship. It is the great emphasis of this passage.

Sonship

What does it mean to be a son of God, and be adopted into his family? We can do no better than give a summary-definition of the doctrine from the famous Westminster Confession, so that we see the teaching as a whole:

> 'All those that are justified, God vouchsafeth, in and for his only Son Jesus Christ, to make partakers of the grace of adoption: by which they are taken into the number, and enjoy the liberties and privileges of the children of God; have his name put upon them, receive the Spirit of adoption; have access to the throne of grace with bold-ness; are enabled to cry, Abba, Father; are pitied, protected, provided for, and chastened by him as by a father; yet never cast off, but sealed to the day of redemp-tion, and inherit the promises, as heirs of everlasting salvation.' (Chapter XII).

Clearly this is a matter of *status* or *standing*, something which, unlike our actual state and condition, is fixed and unchangeable; it never varies. Those who are parents know that however much their child's behaviour may vary, nothing can alter the relationship between them. The Apostle John expresses it perfectly in those well-known words in the first chapter of his Gospel.

He begins with what, in many ways, are the saddest words in the Bible. Speaking of the Lord Jesus Christ, he says: 'He came to that which was his own, but his own did not receive him' (verse eleven) – the supreme tragedy of Jewish unbelief.

But the saddest words in the Bible are immediately followed by the gladdest! – 'Yet to all who received him...he gave the right (or authority) to become children of God.' That right is an equal right, common to all the members of the family. There is parity, an equality of status in the sight of God, whatever differences there may be in terms of spiritual maturity and growth in grace. In the words of the Apostle Paul to the Galatians: 'You are all sons of God through faith in Christ Jesus' (3:26).

No degrees

Of course, the difference between the Son of God, the Lord Jesus Christ, and us Christians, is that he is the eternal Son by nature, the second person of the Holy Trinity; whereas we are adopted children. But even the youngest and weakest believer is as much a son of God as the Apostle Paul. Indeed, a Christian is as much a child of God the moment they believe, as they ever will be throughout the countless ages of eternity. True, they will be a sinless son then, whereas he is a sinful son here, but in both situations, they are a son, no more and no less; nothing and no one can alter that.

Even the Prodigal son never ceased to be so during his time in 'the far country', though he disgraced the family name. 'Dear friends,' says John in his first letter, 'now we are children of God...' (3:2). Although we are not yet fully conformed to the likeness of him who is the firstborn among many brothers, and although we need to grow in the family likeness, the standing and privileges of this relationship never change. There are no degrees of sonship. However, we can, and should develop in our understanding and appreciation of the status conferred upon us. That is the burden of John's statement at the beginning of chapter three in his first letter: 'How great is the love the Father has lavished on us, that we should be called children of God! And that is what we are!...' If only we realized this, most of our spiritual problems would be solved. But our grasp of what is involved, and the status itself, are two very different things.

Cannot be broken

It is very important that we are clear about this distinction, because it has a direct bearing on our personal assurance as believers. Adoption into the family of God is similar to justification by faith. Justification is not a process, but an act in which, for the sake of Christ, God pronounces us righteous. It is a declaration on his part as to how he views us. Adoption is like that. Once it is bestowed upon us, it admits of no variation or change, even when we act 'out of character'. To use the obvious example; when a child disobeys his parents he is a naughty child, but he does not cease to be a child, or even become any less of a child. The relationship, by definition, cannot be broken.

SONSHIP A DISTINCTIVE BLESSING

This needs to be stressed because some theologians (e.g. Louis Berkhof, in his *Systematic Theology*) have discussed the grace of adoption as if it were only one aspect of the new standing granted to us by justification. But sonship is distinct from, and additional to, the other blessings of salvation, and it carries with it its own unique and special privileges. This is not to say that sonship can ever exist independently of those other blessings – it cannot – but it does mean that it can be distinguished from them.

Think of it like this: take a glorious range of mountains like the Himalayas; made up of different peaks, such as Everest,

Kanchenjungha, K2, and the rest, each of which can be differentiated from the others, and bears its own distinctive name. But in another sense, all those different peaks go together, because they belong to the same great mountain range. It is the same in the much more wonderful realm of salvation. No one is ever adopted into the family of God who is not at the same time born again and justified. And yet, that act by which a person becomes a son of God is quite distinct from every other blessing.

SONSHIP AN EXCLUSIVE BLESSING

It belongs only to a unique and special body of people – those who, realizing their own helplessness and hopelessness as the result of sin, believe on the Lord Jesus Christ as Saviour, and are relying only and entirely on his death for their acceptance with God and their hope of heaven.

Two religions

This is something about which we need to be crystal clear. One of the fundamental tenets of theological liberalism is its belief in the 'universal Fatherhood of God', and the 'universal brotherhood of man'. But as Gresham Machen has demonstrated so cogently in his book of the same title, Christianity and Liberalism are two entirely different religions.[2] Nowhere does the difference become more apparent than at this very point.

The Bible patently does not teach the universal Fatherhood of God and the universal brotherhood of man, except in the very limited sense that God has created all men, and by nature we are all one in sin. As Paul put it to the Athenians, in his great address before the Areopagus, '...We are his offspring' (Acts 17:28). But the dreadful reality is that as the result of sin and the Fall, we are all like those unbelieving Jews, of whom our Lord said on one occasion, 'You belong to your father, the devil, and you want to carry out your father's desire...' (John 8:44).

However, the glory of the gospel lies in the fact that it takes those who were, as Paul reminded the Ephesians, 'the children

of disobedience...' and therefore, '...the children of wrath...'
(2:2, 3 KJV), and adopting them into the family of God, imparts
to them a new nature, and makes them his children. Sonship,
then, is not a universal status, but a redemptive privilege, exclu-
sive to these people, and to these alone.

SONSHIP THE SUPREME BLESSING

'How great is the love the Father has lavished on us, that we
should be called children of God! And that is what we are!...'
(1 John 3:1). John had seen the marvel and wonder of his
position, was rejoicing in it, and wanted his readers to do the
same. There is nothing beyond this! Going back to the illustration of the Himalayas – this is the 'Everest' of the whole range;
the topmost pinnacle of Christian privilege, the greatest blessing
that salvation affords, higher and more glorious even than justification.

Justification is certainly the *basic* and *foundational* blessing
of the gospel, because it puts us right with God. But sonship
goes well beyond it, because of the deeper and richer relationship that is involved. The difference is this: justification is a legal
standing, and concerns the standing of an accused man before
the judge. Sonship though, goes much higher, because this
concerns the relationship of a child with its parent.

We can think of the difference like this: by the matchless grace
of God, through faith, we have been restored to the Father's
house. The foundation of that house, the whole basis of our
acceptance, is justification by the blood of Christ.

The top rung

But there is more to a house than its foundations – even though
they are essential. There in the rooms above the foundation,
and resting securely upon it, family life goes on; family relation-
ships – especially the relationship of the children with their
father. That is sonship according to the New Testament! Here
we come to the very apex of grace and of privilege, the top rung

of the ladder of salvation. As we have seen, the Apostle John never got tired of this, as none of us will, because eternity itself will not exhaust the wonder of it. The question is; have we seen it? Are we thrilled by the thought of it? Has it led to abounding praise?

> Children of the heavenly King,
> As ye journey, sweetly sing.
> *John Cennick*

The more one considers this, and what is involved, the more staggering it becomes. And yet that is the truth about every believer, no matter how humble. Surely, there is no greater tragedy than for Christians to think of the blessings of salvation only in terms of forgiveness, vital though that is.

But having considered the doctrine of sonship, and the wonder of the spiritual status which is ours in Christ, we need to look at some of the implications of this great truth, because there is so much rich teaching here.

Privileges

To begin with, think of the enormous privileges of this position. One can illustrate the point very easily. As we know, the general rule in life is that the higher a man's status, or standing in society, the greater the privileges granted to him; although sometimes that principle has been taken to ridiculous lengths. Years ago, I remember a friend, who worked in the British Civil Service, telling me that when a person was upgraded, he or she was not only given a bigger desk, but a different type of waste-paper receptacle! If I recall correctly the lower grade clerical officers had metal ones, while the higher grade were granted wickerwork containers! As the New Testament makes clear, adoption into the family of God takes us right to the top of the ladder of spiritual privilege – there is no higher 'grade' possible. But the glory of that exalted status is matched by the greatness of its privileges. Think of what that entails!

John Owen, often called the 'Prince of the Puritans', describes sonship as 'our fountain privilege'. That is a perfect illustration because every other privilege and blessing flows from the fact that I am his child. And because of the kind of Father that he is, there is nothing that he will not do for me, provided it is for my true well-being. It is all so wonderfully summarised in that statement in the Westminster Confession. Go over it, phrase by phrase. It can be summarized as this: everything is catered for in this life, whatever comes to meet us, and whatever emergency we may have to face. When trials come and –

> When all things seem against us,
> To drive us to despair,
> We know one gate is open,
> One ear will hear our prayer.
> *Oswald Allen*

As my heavenly Father he knows exactly what my needs are, and every provision that is needful is guaranteed. It does not matter what the problem is – especially when trouble comes – I can be sure that he knows all about it. We have all seen this kind of incident, have we not? A little child is playing, skipping about with not a care in the world. But what does the child do when it falls over and grazes its knee? They immediately run back to the parent for comfort. What does the parent then say? 'I'll kiss it better.' And of course, it does feel better! Why? – Because that child has been reassured of the parent's love and concern. It is the same in the spiritual realm. Whatever happens, whatever the problem, our heavenly Father is always there, waiting and ready to receive us, and give us the comfort we need.

To change the illustration: the Managing Director of a big company may be too busy to speak to one of his staff, but he will always find time if one of his children urgently needs to see him. Whenever I go to my heavenly Father, I can be sure of immediate access into his presence, and the certainty of receiving his personal attention and concern. How wonderful it all is!

Whatever it takes

A further implication is that as sons, we can therefore expect to receive the Father's discipline: for the reason that with the privileges go the responsibilities. The proof that the Father really loves his children and not just indulges them (though he does that), is that he will want the very best for them. It means he will train them, and apply discipline, when necessary.

As we know from our own childhood, children often misinterpret a firm discipline, as if it means that their father is against them. Christians sometimes feel that way, but they should not. As our text reminds us, it is those whom the Lord loves that he disciplines. In one sense chastisement is the greatest privilege of all, because when I go astray, he is committed to bringing me back. And he is prepared to use any means necessary – whatever it takes – to do so. He is preparing me for a glorious destiny to come, and he has determined to get me there.

So, far from complaining at his dealings with us, we should rejoice in them, as a further evidence of our adoption. The hymn says, 'O Love, that wilt not let me go!' – even though at times we almost wish it would, to leave us free to go our own way.

We can fitly close this chapter with some questions: Do you know God as your heavenly Father, through Christ? Do you remind yourself daily of the relationship? Is the family likeness increasingly apparent in your life? When Charles Wesley found Christ (or was found by him) on Whit-Sunday, 1738, his experience overflowed into verse:

> O how I shall the goodness tell,
> Father, which Thou to me hast showed?
> That I, a child of wrath and hell,
> I should be called a child of God,
> Should know, should feel my sins forgiven,
> Blest with this antepast (foretaste) of heaven!

Do those words find an echo in your heart?

| **7** | **son-training** |

'And you have forgotten that word of encouragement that addresses you as sons: "My son, do not make light of the Lord's discipline, and do not lose heart when he rebukes you, because the Lord disciplines those he loves, and he punishes everyone he accepts as a son."'

Hebrews 12:5-6

As we have already established in previous chapters the recipients of this great letter were going through a period of great discouragement – largely, it seems, because of the trials they were undergoing. But according to the author of Hebrews, the reason why these people were so cast down by their afflictions is because they had completely misunderstood the situation in which they found themselves. Far from implying that God was against them, the hardship these believers were experiencing really meant precisely the opposite. It demonstrated that he was a true Father to them – by dealing with them as good fathers always will deal with their sons – they will discipline them.

What is best

The reason why these Hebrews had misread the situation was because they had lost touch with their very own Scriptures such as the one quoted here, (Prov. 3:12) where God makes it abundantly clear that as our heavenly Father, he knows exactly what we need, and what is best for us. Consequently, we can expect him to exercise discipline over our lives, and even at times to chastise us severely, in order to keep us in line with his will; or if we have gone astray, to restore us. Discipline, though painful, is always administered in love, with our best interests at heart, and above all, to prepare us for the glorious destiny ahead. The problem with these people, as with all of us at times, was their failure to grasp the marvel and wonder of their standing in God's sight, as his children. Having the best Father, and the most faithful, we must expect to be disciplined.

A query

The recurrent theme running through this whole section is that if we are not conscious of being dealt with, it inevitably raises a query against our whole position – as to whether we are children of God at all! After all, why does God bother with us – why does he not just leave us to go our own self-indulgent way? It is for the same reason that any father worthy of the name will discipline his children – because he loves them and desires the very best for them.

The person who ought to be most suspicious of himself is the one who is not aware of being disciplined in any sense. He ought to feel alarmed. Arthur W. Pink states in his usual direct manner (though none the worse for that): 'Woe to the man whom God chastens not, whom he allows to go recklessly on in the boastful and presumptuous security which so many now mistake for faith. There is a reckoning to come of which he little dreams.'[1] Discipline is a proof and a demonstration of parental love, and if we are not conscious of ever being 'at the receiving end', and that does not awaken us to examine our whole position, we are fools. So we need to consider this matter very carefully.

THE ESSENTIAL CHARACTER OF SON-TRAINING

If we are not clear on this, we shall misunderstand the whole doctrine, and miss the main thrust of the argument. Furthermore, it will lead to further discouragement.

Those readers, who are more familiar with the King James Version (AV), will see that that term translated as 'discipline' in the NIV is rendered as 'chastening', or 'chastisement', by the older version. However, although the AV translation is not actually wrong, it can be misleading. The modern rendering conveys the writer's intended meaning far more accurately at this point. It does so because when we hear or read the word chastisement, we immediately think of a father punishing his child for a particular misdemeanour – perhaps an act of disobedience. Although that element is included in the notion of discipline, as we will see that is not the main emphasis here. The word in the original Greek literally means 'child-training'. It means to educate, to rear, to mentor, and to discipline a child, with all that this involves. The word used here has a much wider scope that what we tend to think of as 'chastisement'.

Child training may well include rebuke and correction – it may even involve severe punishment at times, but it is by no means confined to that aspect.

This is a much bigger thing altogether, and covers everything that goes under the heading of child- rearing. So it includes instruction and direction in life as well – everything that is needed to produce spiritual maturity. Not only that; it seems clear from this letter that one of the main troubles with these Hebrew Christians was their failure to distinguish between the retributive anger of God, and the fatherly discipline of God. There is a huge difference between them so, unless we have grasped this vital point, we too will be confused.

Once and forever

The reality is that no child of God can ever suffer the sanctions of the broken law and be punished for sin in a penal sense. God, the Judge Eternal, has already punished those sins in Jesus Christ on the cross, and dealt with them once and forever. There, on Calvary's hill, in the flowing blood and crimson lines of that terrible, yet glorious death, our Saviour took the guilt of our sins upon himself. As our divinely-appointed substitute, he suffered the full judgement of God upon those sins – past, present, and even future!

The implication is clear. If our sins have already been condemned and punished in him, for God to punish them again would be an act of injustice, for –

> Payment God cannot twice demand,
> First at my bleeding Surety's hand,
> And then again at mine.
> *A.M. Toplady*

But, while it remains true that the Christian cannot ever be condemned by God as judge, he can, and will be disciplined by God as Father, because that is fundamental to the parent-child relationship.

A new relationship

As believers therefore, we are now in an entirely different position to the one we were in before we believed. A Christian is not just someone whose sins have been forgiven. He *has* been forgiven, and that is marvellous good news. But something still more wonderful has taken place. He has been adopted into the family of God, – an entirely new relationship has come into being.

Because of that new, filial relationship, a child of God can expect to be brought up in the *ways* of God. Children need instruction, training and discipline; they need reproof and admonition – and at times, alas, they need the smack of chastisement. Even then, the punishment is only ever remedial, not retributive. And it is always administered in love, not in wrath. Psalm eighty-nine, which is clearly Messianic, puts it like this: 'If his sons forsake my law and do not follow my statutes, if they violate my decrees and fail to keep my commands, I will punish their sin with the rod, their iniquity with flogging; but I will not

take my love from him, nor will I ever betray my faithfulness'
(verses 30-33). The relationship in all this is therefore crucial,
not only to an understanding of the teaching here, but to all of
God's dealings with us.

Discipline may cause us to smart, but we must always bear
in mind that our heavenly Father is only correcting and not con-
demning. He is not smiting in wrath, but only training in love.
Indeed, discipline is one of the greatest blessings in the Christian life. Where would we be without it?

> How oft to sure destruction
> Our feet had gone astray,
> Wert Thou not, patient Shepherd,
> The Guardian of our way.
> *Laurence Tuttiett*

Chastisement then, whatever form it takes, proceeds from the
love and faithfulness of an all-wise heavenly Father. Have we
realized that? Can you honestly thank God for times of affliction, because it brought you back to him, or drew you closer? In
the words of Thomas Brooks, the Puritan: 'Can you look through
the darkest cloud, and see God smiling at you?'

Too loving

When things go wrong, do you still tend to say (as the unbeliever does), 'What have I done to deserve this? Why am I having
such a hard time of it, when others seem to be having such an
easy life?' If you do react to trials in that way (as discouraged
Christians can), it means you have forgotten what a unique and
special relationship you now enjoy with God. You need to
examine your own foundations, to see whether you really are a
child of God! With the Psalmist, the true saint should say this, 'It
was good for me to be afflicted so that I might learn your
decrees' (Ps. 119:71). He thanks God for trials because he knows
that nothing happens to the Christian by chance. Everything

comes from the hand of his heavenly Father, who is too loving not to discipline his erring child, and too wise to make a mistake in how he does so.

A heavy trial or affliction is not necessarily a chastisement for falling into particular sin. This is why it is so important for us to understand the doctrine of son-training, because if a Christian falls into the trap of thinking that every time he is in trouble, it must be because he has displeased God, and grieved the Holy Spirit, that can only lead to great spiritual discouragement, not to say depression.

BASIC CONSTITUENTS IN SON-TRAINING

These are not absolute, watertight distinctions, because they obviously overlap at some points. However, to divide it up like this should help to clarify our thinking.

1. There is what we might describe as **vindicative** discipline. The classic example of this is found in the life of Job. Doubtless he derived much instruction and correction from the terrible experiences through which he passed. But in the words of Professor John Murray, '...the key to the interpretation of Job's sufferings is not divine chastisement upon Job for sins that he had committed, but rather the challenge that was made by Satan in...the unseen realm.'[2]

Satan appeared before God, and said, 'Does Job fear God for nothing?' The innuendo was that Job's godly and upright life was motivated solely by what he got out of it – especially his temporal prosperity. In other words, Job was godly because it paid him to be so. The challenge to God implicit in that devilish insinuation could not go unanswered. It was a lie, and because God knew it was, he allowed Satan to buffet Job, in order to demonstrate to men and angels that Job's integrity and piety was truly disinterested, and independent of earthly prosperity.

The lesson ought to be obvious. To quote John Murray again, '...we do well to avoid the rash conclusion, too often indulged

in, that sufferings visited upon God's people are direct visita-
tions of the divine displeasure upon them for sins that we
think…that they have committed.'[3]

It was Job's miserable 'comforters', so-called, who took it for
granted that because he had suffered in such a terrible way, it
must be because he had sinned grievously. But they were wrong,
and finally Job was vindicated. So too was God, because he
knew that his servant would not fail the test. So the devil was
put to flight. Vindicative discipline! – No doubt it still happens,
although the ways of God in this respect are shrouded in
mystery and 'his footsteps are not known'. As Shakespeare puts
it, 'There are more things in heaven and earth than are dreamt
of in your philosophy, Horatio.' (Hamlet).

Hidden purposes

What is certain is that God's purposes in permitting affliction
may, for a long time, be hidden from the believer concerned.
Indeed, they may never know in this life why certain trials are
visited upon them. As the Lord said to Peter in a different context: 'You do not realize now what I am doing, but later
(hereafter?) you will understand' (John 13:7). As our heavenly
Father has assured us that whatever happens, it will work for
our good, our part is to exercise patience, and in all things to
submit to his will without murmuring and complaining:

> Whate'er my God ordains is right:
> Here shall my stand be taken;
> Though sorrow, need, or death be mine,
> Yet am I not forsaken.
> My Father's care
> Is round me there;
> He holds me that I shall not fall:
> And so to him I leave it all.
> *Samuel Rodigast*

2. There is **instructive** discipline, by which is meant that as our teacher and mentor, our heavenly Father's basic method in raising his children, and bringing them to maturity, is by means of positive instruction. Our Lord prayed for his own to that end: 'Sanctify them by the truth; your word is truth' (John 17:17). It is the same at the natural level; we know that our children need to be educated, or need to be taught the basic disciplines at the very least.

Apply that to the spiritual realm and the Christian life. As our heavenly Father, God does not begin with lines, or detention, or, as we had in my school-days, the cane! – any more than an earthly teacher would. He begins rather with positive instruction, teaching us about himself and the great doctrines of the faith, and their practical implications for our lives. 'Your word is a lamp to my feet and a light for my path', says the Psalmist (Ps. 119:105), and that is why Christians delight to spend time in studying these glorious truths. That is also why the writer to the Hebrews has to call his readers back to the Scriptures.

However, positive instruction is only a part of son-training. Our Father would prefer it to be the main part, but we, like all children, do not give sufficient attention to the teaching we are given. We neglect or disobey the Word, so God has to 'turn the sound up', as it were, and use other means to get through to us.

3. There is **corrective** or **restorative** discipline. Every parent will know immediately what this means. You begin by giving your child positive instruction and direction. If they deliberately disobey and fail to profit from teaching, then you have to employ other means of discipline which are more painful. Not surprisingly, the child will not take kindly to this, at least not initially. As this man puts it in verse eleven, 'No discipline seems pleasant at the time.' But it is very necessary, and the parents who truly love their children will not shrink from giving it.

Again, that is analogous to what happens in the spiritual realm. Our Father in heaven is like that; so when we refuse to listen to his Word, are stubborn and self-willed, we should not

be surprised when he takes us in hand, and uses stronger methods
to bring us to our senses. Be sure of this, he will deal with us,
and it can be a very unpleasant process indeed. Thank God, he
is 'slow to anger,' and 'does not treat us as our sins deserve'
(Ps. 103:8,10). There are many failings and weaknesses he graciously overlooks. If he did not, if he 'kept a record of sins…who
could stand?' (Ps. 130:3). We would be under his frown and
displeasure all the time.

But there are some things which, as a good Father, he cannot overlook. Things will begin to go wrong in our lives, which
cause us distress and pain. It can be almost anything; a disappointment of some kind, some castle or other we have been
building up there in the stratosphere comes crashing about our
ears; trouble with other people, problems at work, domestic
upheaval, illness – the list is endless. Once we begin to realize
this, it enables us to understand many things in life which otherwise would be a complete mystery. But it is all part of our Father's
educational policy for his children; that great plan and purpose
to prepare and fit them for the glorious future he has in mind for
them – and he will stop at nothing to bring us to that.

Short-changing God

As we have seen, that does not mean that every trouble is to be
interpreted as a measure of corrective discipline for a particular
sin. These categories overlap: but it may be the explanation. So
whenever anything unpleasant takes place in our circumstances,
our immediate reaction ought to be: 'Maybe I needed that. Have
I been getting slack? Am I short-changing God in some area or
other? Has a degree of carelessness and indiscipline crept into
my Christian life? Is there some sin not repented of?'

How can we know whether this is the case or not? In general
the answer is fairly self-evident. What kind of a father would he
be, who when his son asked him why he had felt the sting of his
hand upon his anatomy, refused to tell him? Our Father has his
own ways of letting us know he has a controversy with us –

either through conscience, or the Word, or by means of a brotherly admonition (Job 10:2; Ps. 139:23).

4. This can be described as **formative** or **productive** discipline. We have a perfect instance of this in our Lord's 'parable' or illustration of the vine in John 15:1-3. Sometimes, when you see a horticulturist pruning a fruit tree right back, you think that they are going too far and will kill it. But, if they know their job, this heavy pruning is quite deliberate; for the aim is always to increase the crop and produce more and better fruit.

Paul makes the same point. He says that the believer can actually rejoice in sufferings, because he knows that suffering produces perseverance, character, and hope (Rom. 5:3-4). In this sense, the more the child of God brings forth the fruit of the Spirit, the more he will be aware of discipline, to enable him to produce more fruit! That is why some of the godliest men who have ever lived have experienced such terrible trials.

5. The final element we can call **preventative** discipline. Our Father's discipline is not only corrective, to restore us from sin, but anticipatory, to prevent us falling into it.

The greatest example of this principle is found in what Paul recounts of his own experience in 2 Corinthians, chapter 12. He tells us of how he had been caught up to the third heaven, and given amazing revelations and visions. The danger then for the great apostle was pride. The Lord knew this, so he was sent a thorn in the flesh – not because he had become proud, but in order to humble him, and keep him from pride. Spiritual and intellectual pride is a terrible danger, especially to those who know a little theology. Sometimes, in our folly, we think we know it all, and become smug and self-satisfied. Paul had not fallen into that trap yet, so the Lord gives him a dose of preventative medicine – a prophylactic – to keep him from it. 'Great God of wonders, all thy ways are matchless...'

We cannot conclude this chapter without noting the wonderful personal condescension of God in all this. It is brought out by the word rendered as 'addresses' in verse five: '...you have forgotten that word... that addresses you as sons.' However, 'addresses' is not quite true to the original. The Revised Version of 1881-1885 is more accurate: '...you have forgotten the word... that reasons with you as sons.' When you are training very young children, you do not reason with them, do you? – because they are not old enough to understand. You simply tell them what is right (or wrong, as the case may be), whether they can grasp your reasoning or not. But although God is so far above us, and has a perfect right just to lay down the law and tell us how to behave, without giving his reasons, or indeed any explanation, he does not do so. He comes right down to our level, stoops to our weakness, and treating us as grown-up sons he appeals to our understanding and reasons with us person-to-person, as it were. And in doing so, he pays us a great compliment.

Humbled himself

None of this should surprise us, for this is the God who, in the person of his beloved Son, came down and humbled himself to the death of the cross for our sakes. This is the God who condescends even to say this to sinful men and women, 'Come now, let us reason together... Though your sins are like scarlet, they shall be as white as snow...' (Isaiah 1:18).

Thank God, we are all in his hands,

> Till all life's discipline shall cease,
> And we go home to Thee.
> *Anon., New Congregational Hymn Book, 1859*

8 | losing heart

'And you have forgotten that word of encouragement that addresses you as sons: "My son, do not make light of the Lord's discipline, and do not lose heart when he rebukes you, because the Lord disciplines those he loves, and he punishes everyone he accepts as a son."'

Hebrews 12:5-6

In the previous chapter, we considered the various *forms* of discipline through which our heavenly Father puts us in *this* life as his way of training us up for the life *to come*. The closing words were these: 'Thank God, we are all in his hands, "till all life's discipline shall cease, and we go home to Thee."' Just two days after that message was originally preached my wife had a dreadful accident in which she sustained serious and multiple injuries, leaving her permanently disabled.

This is mentioned for one reason only – to remind us that the issues we are dealing with here are not matters to be handled and discussed in a detached and theoretical manner. Rather, they have tremendous practical relevance to our lives in this world.

As the poet Longfellow put it: 'Life is real, life is earnest...' and, although no doubt we all agree with that sentiment intellectually, sometimes it is not until we actually meet up with serious trouble, either in our own life, or in the life of someone near and dear to us, that we realize just *how* real and earnest it is.

However, as the Apostle Paul reminds the Corinthians, 'No temptation (or trial) has seized you except what is common to man. And God is faithful; he will not let you be tempted (or tried) beyond what you can bear. But when you are tempted, he will also provide a way out so that you can stand up under it.' (1 Cor. 10:13).

The grand purpose

But the main way in which God enables us to bear trials is by what Paul again refers to as '…the encouragement of the Scriptures…' (Rom.15:4). It works like this. Here in the Scriptures, and especially the New Testament letters, we are taught the grand *purpose* of trials – that they are a part of this great plan of God to sanctify his beloved people and prepare them for glory. So we should thank God for such teaching because it reminds us that, as Paul again writes to the Philippians: '…he who began a good work in you will carry it on to completion until the day of Christ Jesus.' (Phil. 1:6).

This is why the Scriptures do not just *sympathize* with those who are passing through deep waters. It gives them *doctrine* – it spells out the reasons *why* God permits what to the unbeliever is unmitigated disaster. And here in the twelfth chapter of Hebrews we are given that teaching in an exceptionally clear form, in the doctrine of adoption, or sonship, with its inevitable corollary of discipline and chastisement.

Practical

In reading these New Testament letters then, one is made continually aware of the *practical* intent with which they were written. There are vast, soaring thoughts here, 'infinities and immensities', as Thomas Carlyle put it, that will tax the redeemed mind to the limit. But these letters were invariably sent because of a situation that had arisen among the Christians concerned – some problem, or problems, that needed to be addressed. They were penned always out of a burning concern to help and encourage the believers concerned. That is especially true of this particular passage. However, the reason why God the Holy Spirit caused these letters to be written, was not only to deal with that immediate and local situation in the first century, but to instruct and edify the people of God in every age and generation, hence our present consideration of these vital matters.

It is a simple truism – though we need reminding of it – that whatever century we live in, whatever type of culture and society, and whatever our own peculiar circumstances, the Christian life is essentially the same; and therefore our basic problems remain the same.

Here, the writer to the Hebrews deals with an ever-recurring problem in the Christian life – the very real problem of discouragement. Who among us has not suffered from this – perhaps in an acute form? Maybe this is true of you now. So we need to look at this issue.

THE CONDITION ITSELF

Notice how it is put. 'And you have forgotten that word of encouragement that addresses you as sons…' The very fact that these folk had forgotten the Scriptural encouragement in the trying situation in which they found themselves, clearly implies that they had become discouraged.

We get the same thing further on in verse five, where, quoting from the book of Proverbs (3:11,12), readers are exhorted not to 'lose heart'. In a poem entitled *Gold Scar*, Amy Carmichael wrote: 'Hast thou no scar? No hidden scar on foot, or hand, or side?…Can he have followed far, who has no wound or scar?'

Sooner or later every Christian experiences affliction and trouble in their lives, and the lasting pain and stress that often accompanies it. Life is difficult at the best of times for us all, but as the result of unusual trials, many believers are especially vulnerable to discouragement. We all recognize 'the walking wounded' in our churches and need to accept that Christians too become depressed, even cynical (though they should not), and some suffer breakdowns.

Some are more prone to this, but surely we are all aware of the condition? It is that spiritual and even physical state of apathy and listlessness into which, for one reason or another, we have fallen. Our spirits droop and flag, our zeal evaporates, and we just cannot be bothered to rouse ourselves and make an effort. As a consequence everything becomes a drag and a burden – indeed there are times when we could hardly care less whether we went on or not, with the inevitable drop in personal standards that follows. We can all recognize ourselves here – how well the Scriptures know us!

Discouraged

However, this problem of discouragement is very subtle. Half the battle is getting us to face up to what is happening, and to examine ourselves. Generally speaking, unless they are psychological masochists, people do not get into this state *deliberately* and in a calculated manner, as we go into some sins. As we saw in chapter five on *Spiritual Amnesia*, the reason why we succumb to discouragement is, as the writer reminds us, because we have not applied the Scriptures to our lives!

We have to face up to this, not only because discouragement makes us miserable and unhappy and ruins our assurance, but also because a discouraged Christian is of very little *practical* use in the work of the Kingdom, and in Christian witness.

The condition described here is a very common one; particularly it seems, at the present time. In the words of Dr. Martyn Lloyd-Jones: 'If I were asked to hazard an opinion as to what is the most prevailing disease in the Church today I would suggest that it is discouragement.'[1] That was said in 1960, over forty years ago, but if Dr. Lloyd-Jones was correct in his diagnosis *then*, surely the symptoms of this condition are even more evident *today*. A contemporary writer has put it similarly: 'One of the saddest features of the life of the Church is the widespread prevalence of a spirit of discouragement.'

Always hope

At this point we are not so much concerned with the *causes* of discouragement as the *reality* of it in our Christian experience. Anyone who knows their Bible will have come across it frequently, especially in the book of Psalms. In Psalms 42 and 43 the psalmist again and again addresses his own soul and questions himself: 'Why are you downcast, O my soul? Why so disturbed within me?' (42:5,11; 43:5). How honest the psalmist is! He freely confesses to being in this condition – and that is good. There is always hope for such a person because admitting one's depression is the prerequisite to getting out of it. But that state of soul was not confined to believers under the old dispensation.

These New Testament saints were also in this condition, so the idea that after Pentecost believers were always on the mountaintop, overflowing with assurance and joy, is not true. What was the problem with these Hebrews? We have already established in previous chapters that the main reason why these people were dispirited and cast down was because they did not trust the promises of God. The question came to them, 'What is the point of it all?'

A setback

We have all known those times when after a setback, the thought enters our mind, 'Why go on? What is the use? Where is it all getting me?' There is no doubt that at that point, we don't *feel* like going on. We feel like giving up! There is only one thing that will hold us at such times; it is this glorious word of encouragement that we find here in the Scriptures. God's Word is '...a lamp to my feet and light for our path' (Psalm 119:105).

THE CAUSES OF DISCOURAGEMENT

The causes of discouragement can be any one of a number of

things, or indeed, a combination of factors. In one sense, there is no need to go into a detailed description of the things that cause a Christian to lose heart; their number is legion! Whatever the particular reason may be, the way in which Scripture deals with it is essentially the same for all of us. So if anyone is saying, 'But you do not know what I have had to endure', it means that you have not understood the Scriptures properly. We are told in 1 Corinthians 10:13: 'No trial has seized you except what is common to man.' There are no exceptions that are not covered. This speaks to every one of us, whatever form our trouble may take. The first step in dealing with this unhappy condition is to recognize it for what it is, and then to ask ourselves what is causing the problem.

What is the problem?

We have already seen how the psalmist speaks to himself in Psalm 42 and 43. 'Come along now,' he says, 'why are you like this? – what is the matter with you?' We have to do that – talk to ourselves and take ourselves in hand. But although the Bible does deal with the problem of discouragement by giving us general principles which apply to us all, whatever our individual circumstances, it is important that, as the psalmist did, I pinpoint the particular reason why I am cast down. Having done that and isolated the problem, I face it and see how the Scriptural teaching applies to that particular problem, and to me personally.

Although we cannot enumerate all the possible sources of discouragement, what we can do is try and identify some of the *main* causes of the problem; to help us in recognizing what *our* condition stems from. It may well be that your problem, or problems, are completely different to those that confronted these Hebrews. But whatever the difficulty is, it is all part of life in God's preparatory school, in which our heavenly Father is training us up for heaven.

We can conveniently divide up these causes of discouragement under two headings, *general*, and *particular*.

The general causes of discouragement

1. Temperament causing depression

We need first to recognize that this is a syndrome to which some people are especially prone, both by nature and disposition. They cannot help that, of course, because they are *born* like it, and the *new birth* does not basically change this tendency. It is a matter of temperament that can make them more subject to depression than those whose temperament is more equable and phlegmatic. So the first thing we must do is to *know ourselves*, and if we discern a constitutional weakness in this direction, we need to be on the watch for it, and put a guard up at certain points. For instance, some people tend to go down in spirit because of something as simple as getting insufficient sleep. It can be as basic as that!

2. The whole state of the world, and the state of the Church

This general cause of discouragement is particularly prevalent today, especially in Britain. There is no doubt that we are living in very dark, and therefore discouraging days. As we look around us and hear the news, we see evil and sin so powerfully organized, and so deeply entrenched – with the people of God apparently ineffective in stemming the tide – it is small wonder that those who stand for truth and righteousness should be disheartened. Not only is it 'a day of small things', but the devil seems unusually active and there is terrible confusion everywhere. In Shakespeare's words: 'Chaos has come again.' It has never been easy to be a Christian, but it seems particularly difficult at the present time, largely because of the fearful decline in faith and morals witnessed in our lifetime.

Particular forms of discouragement

We move on to some of the more particular forms of discouragement that result from our personal state and circumstances.

1. A consciousness of failure

When this is prevalent in the Christian life it results in an acute sense of unworthiness. We may be quite clear on the doctrine of justification by faith alone, and we know and believe that 'If we confess our sins, he is faithful and just and will forgive us our sins and purify us from all unrighteousness' (1 John 1:9). But what gets us down are these continual failures and defeats – and the 'leaden-eyed despairs', as the poet Keats so feelingly put it, that inevitably follow. It seems that far from making progress in the Christian life, we are going backwards. How common this is.

2. A sense of personal inadequacy in God's service

Strange to say this discouragement can stem from engaging in an activity which everyone agrees is good for us – namely the reading of Christian biography. We can read about the lives of even ordinary men and women – in the Puritan era, say – and compared to their godliness it seems as if we have hardly begun! This is especially true of preachers. For example, if we read the life of C.H. Spurgeon, and find that in the first seven years of his ministry in London he preached on average ten times a week, the thought can come: 'If that is what it means to be a Christian minister, what about me?' The immediate reaction is to feel you have done nothing and achieved nothing. It can cause us to lose heart and feel practically useless, even though we try to tell ourselves that we were never meant to be someone else, and that even one-talent preachers have a part to play in the great crusade for God and truth.

3. Being weary and tired in the little that one is doing

'Let us not become weary in doing good...', says Paul to the Galatians (6:9), but so often we are just that, worn out – or so it feels. The sheer strain and complexity of life in the modern world is being increasingly recognized – and that is apart from 'the daily round and common task' that forms such a large part of our lives.

In addition, so much of our general church life seems ordinary and humdrum. Little appears to be happening and the services seem so unexciting compared to the wonderful things that took place in former days: particularly days of revival. The feeling creeps in: 'Is it worthwhile carrying on? Is it not time for others to take the strain?' We must ask ourselves honestly how often have we felt like that.

4. Anxiety and fears of one kind or another

These are another prolific cause of discouragement. Worry has been endemic in the human race since the Fall. But because life is so involved nowadays, and the whole pace of life has increased, so have things to worry about; especially with the conscientious, perhaps highly-strung type of person. Then there are fears concerning the future, and what might happen. The result is life becomes a burden because of the multifarious things to worry about!

5. The general 'rough and tumble' of life

This can cause Christians to become dispirited. The unusual trials and temptations; sickness of one kind or another; people who let us down and are difficult to live with; unkind criticism and misunderstandings; disappointments in life – all these things affect us and tend to get us down. There is no end to it in a world like this, whilst we are still in the body. But the Bible not only understands our problems, it deals with them. Here in this verse, we have the final answer to all those questions that instinctively rise up within us at times of perplexity and discouragement.

THE CURE FOR THIS CONDITION

What we need to grasp at the outset is that discouragement is always *wrong*, besides being unnecessary! 'My son...do not lose heart!' This needs to be stated bluntly. The Word of God provides a remedy for *every* spiritual ill but once we justify a spirit of discouragement in ourselves, we are dishonouring it. In effect, we are implying that our circumstances are so unique and special that Scripture does not cover them.

Do not misunderstand this – of course we should sympathize with others in trouble, and if we know ourselves, and our own weakness, we can well understand why some people are cast down. But although our great High Priest sympathizes with our griefs and troubles, as this letter makes so abundantly clear, he never allows us to *wallow* in discouragement and feel sorry for ourselves.

To put it another way, the Bible is never *sentimental*. That comes out very strongly here. As we have seen, the word translated as 'addresses' in verse five would be better rendered as 'reasons'. 'You have forgotten that word...that *reasons* with you as sons.' 'Be logical,' says this man in effect, 'work it out from Scripture. Talk to yourself, remind yourself of the teaching, think through the argument!' When we do, this is what we find:

1. For us!

We see first of all that discipline is an expression of God's *love*, not his *anger*. The reason why all these trials are put upon us is not because God is *against* us, but because he is *for* us. 'The Lord disciplines those he loves!' Or as the Lord says to the Church of the Laodiceans, 'Those whom I *love* I rebuke and discipline...' (Rev. 3:19). These are categorical statements. So, whatever trouble we may be in, we need to hold on to that. We have to resist the devil, who will always suggest the opposite. 'But if God loves me,' says someone, 'why has he allowed all these troubles?' It is because he is determined to bring you to glory! He is carrying forward this process of training and preparation. As a believer, he has loved you with an everlasting love.

> He saw me ruined in the Fall,
> Yet loved me, notwithstanding all.
> *Samuel Medley*

Then, in pursuance of that love, he permitted his dear Son to suffer in a way, and to a degree, that none of us will ever experience – or could.

> See, from his head, his hands, his feet,
> Sorrow and love flow mingled down.
> *Isaac Watts*

Furthermore, he brought you to a personal knowledge and experience of that love.

> Loved with everlasting love,
> Led by grace that love to know.
> *G.W. Robertson*

2. The best

Secondly, discipline is also an expression of true Fatherhood (cf. verses 7 and 8). Any father, who is not a father in *name* only, is going to train and discipline his children, not least because he loves them and wants the best for them! Indeed at times, he has to 'be cruel to be kind', as we say, in their interests. So the cure for 'losing heart' is simply this: when the devil whispers in your ear, 'Why go on? What is the point?' – you turn on him, and say with John Newton:

His love in time past
Forbids me to think
He'll leave me at last
In trouble to sink;
Each sweet Ebenezer
I have in review
Confirms his good pleasure
To help me quite through.

I am in his hands, who has promised never to leave me nor
forsake me, and therefore whatever my lot, 'it is well, it is well,
with my soul'. Richard Baxter put it perfectly:

Christ leads me through no darker rooms
Than he went through before;
And he that to God's kingdom comes
Must enter by this door.

Let us keep our gaze firmly on him, who in spite of everything
that was set against him, was never discouraged – who for the
joy that was set before him, endured even the cross, for our sake.

To feel that though I journey on
By stony paths and rugged ways,
Thy blessèd feet have gone before,
And strength is given for weary days.
                                    Anon.

9 | responding to discipline

'And you have forgotten that word of encouragement that addresses you as sons: "My son, do not make light of the Lord's discipline, and do not lose heart when he rebukes you, because the Lord disciplines those he loves, and he punishes everyone he accepts as a son." Endure hardship as discipline; God is treating you as sons. For what son is not disciplined by his father? If you are not disciplined (and everyone undergoes discipline), then you are illegitimate children and not true sons. Moreover, we have all had human fathers who disciplined us and we respected them for it. How much more should we submit to the Father of our spirits and live!'

Hebrews 12:5-9

Problem of suffering

The whole problem of suffering in the Christian life is dealt with in a particularly striking manner in chapter 12 of Hebrews. The author of this profound letter is writing to these Hebrew Christians out of deep concern for their spiritual condition. They were experiencing great hardships and had lost heart and, instead of experiencing joy in the Christian life, they felt they had incurred God's displeasure and had cut themselves off from his favour.

It seems that the reason *why* these believers had become so despondent by their trials and tribulations was because they had completely misconstrued God's dealings with them. Far from implying that God was *against* them, the hardship and afflictions they were suffering demonstrated – even *proved* – that he was a true Father to them. A good father will discipline his son – and by discipline the writer is clearly not only referring to those occasions when the child commits a particularly serious misdemeanour and has to be chastised for it. That is included but it is not the main emphasis here, which is the general training through which our heavenly Father puts all his children in *this* world – in order to prepare them for the better world *to come.*

Misunderstanding

It is a failure to grasp this which so often leads to a complete misunderstanding of the ways of God; and then almost inevitably to spiritual depression. We need to face up to this because it is one of the most powerful, yet subtle weapons in Satan's armoury. In writing to the Corinthians, Paul says, '...For we are not unaware of his schemes.' (2 Cor. 2:11). Maybe not, but we need reminding of them! If the devil cannot inveigle the Christian into committing gross and outward sins of the flesh, he will try another tack and will tempt the troubled believer with doubts about the goodness and love of God – and the faithfulness of his promises. There are situations when to sight and sense it does seem as if God no longer cares for us – indeed, has completely abandoned us.

Then there are times in which, although the believer concerned does pray for grace to bear the trial which has been laid upon him, the temptation to doubt and to murmur seem more active than ever.

It is just then that we need to be reminded of what the writer to the Hebrews describes as 'the word of encouragement that addresses you as sons', (or better, 'that *reasons* with you as sons'). When you reason with someone your whole aim and intention is that by a process of logical thinking, the person in mind should arrive at the right conclusion. That is what the Holy Spirit is aiming at in his dealings with us.

Word and Spirit

A vital, and a major part of the Spirit's work, is to imbue the believer with fresh courage, (see John 14:15-18). His very name and title imply that. He is the *Paraclete;* literally 'The one called alongside', but more than even that – 'called alongside in order to comfort, strengthen, and encourage.' This is his special office, and he can do what a whole battalion of counsellors, analysts and therapists cannot do; because he always has the right key to unlock our hearts. Where would we be without his ministry, and the assurance he gives us of God's love and concern for us, particularly at times of special need?

However, he imparts the needed encouragement by opening our minds and hearts to his own 'breathed out' words of Scripture; and in particular by enabling us to understand the arguments and reasoning of Scripture, as we see here in Hebrews twelve.

> The Spirit breathes upon the Word,
> And brings the truth to sight.
> *William Cowper*

How different is the Biblical approach to these things from how the world views them. If a Christian is suffering, the New Testament does not merely sympathize and offer vague and cheery words of comfort. Still less does it tell him that things can only get better. That kind of approach often masquerades under the name of Christianity; but in reality it is no more than a mixture of bad psychology, auto-suggestion and sentimentality. The idea is that if you keep telling yourself that things are not as bad as they seem, in the end you will come to believe that! You simply do not find that here, or anything like it. Instead, the author of this letter honestly faces the trials his readers were going through, in all their blackness. But although he is utterly realistic, and does not even attempt to minimise the hurt these people were feeling, he is still able to give them a tremendous word of comfort and encouragement, if only they are prepared to reason out the teaching of Scripture.

The business of preaching

We can truly say that a Christian who is cast down and discouraged because of trials and affliction is not thinking clearly. So the concern of the preacher is not just to make his hearers feel happier. As Dr. Martyn Lloyd-Jones once put it, 'The business of preaching is to teach you to think.' That is precisely what the writer to the Hebrews is doing. It may seem hard at the time, because most of us tend to shy away from hard thinking; but it is the only way to receive true comfort.

Although reasoning from Scripture is an essential prerequisite to a sense of peace and assurance, it is not enough. There is something else. The first step is to *understand* the Biblical doctrine of son-training and chastisement. Then having grasped the teaching, the next step is to *apply* it. Discipline does not work automatically, in and of itself. The mere fact of being disciplined does not necessarily mean we are going to profit from it. There are *wrong* ways of reacting to trials, as well as *right* ways, and we need to know the difference.

THE WRONG WAY TO RESPOND TO DISCIPLINE

From the passage before us, we can see at least three wrong ways of reacting.

1. Do not make light of it.

That is evident in the first part of the quotation from Proverbs chapter three, here in verse five. 'My son, do not *make light* of the Lord's discipline.' To 'make light' of something is to not take it very seriously. It is shrugged off, as if something of little consequence. When trial and trouble come, instead of asking ourselves what our heavenly Father is trying to teach us – have we gone astray somewhere; do we need pulling up? – we as good as take no notice of it. To tell the truth, we are not terribly interested and cannot be bothered to try and understand what the Lord is saying to us.

Common response

This is a very common response to discipline; as those who are parents know only too well. They have witnessed it first hand, at the natural level, in their own children! It is the picture of a child who having received chastisement, puts on an air of affected nonchalance and tries to give the impression that they are not going to allow such a little thing to affect them! Their pride is hurt but stubbornness stops them admitting that discipline was needed. The whole situation is totally down-played.

We have all been like that at times. We have deliberately tried to steel ourselves against the discipline, or attempted to shrug it off. Or perhaps we have plunged into other activities to try and forget that there is even a problem. That is essentially the unbelieving world's reaction, and a child of God who responds in that way is in a very dangerous condition. It may well mean that his Father has to take even sterner measures in order to *make* them pay attention.

But that is not all, because as there is a haughty pride, which *ignores* 'the rod', so there is a foolish faintness, which *collapses* under it.

2. Do not lose heart under it

This we see in the second half of verse five. It is the exact opposite to the first type of response that tries to pass the whole thing off as of no importance. As someone has well put it, 'The hard-hearted steels himself against it, and the faint-hearted reels under it.' With the latter, this is the person who gets so discouraged, by even a word of rebuke, that they immediately feel like giving up the Christian life altogether. Usually, the first thing that goes is attendance at the means of grace such as the Sunday services, Bible studies and prayer meetings, private Bible study and prayer.

Again, doubtless we can recognize this attitude in ourselves, either in the present or from past experience. 'The slings and arrows' of life are raining down upon us, troubles come in troops, and problems and difficulties pile up. It all becomes too much for us and we tell ourselves that we cannot take any more. The result is we give in to despondency, and cease to make any real effort in the Christian life. We feel very hard done by, as if God was treating us unjustly, and being unfair. As with the first case, this too is a perilous state to be in, because a person who has lost all heart under discipline is in no real position to learn from it.

3. Do not become bitter through it

We find this further on in verse fifteen, where we are warned against allowing a 'bitter root' to spring up in our lives. The caution is a salutary one, for there are some poor souls who react to the harsh vicissitudes of life by turning in on themselves and becoming bitter and twisted. There is nothing neither sadder nor more tragic in life than to see this happen.

All the while the sun was shining, and things were going well, these people seemed pleasant and outgoing. But then they experienced some great loss or disappointment in life, and become sour and self-centred – difficult and trying even to those who were longing to help them. The iron entered their souls, and they gave the impression that everything was against them – even, it seems, God himself. They appeared to be completely different people to what they were before. This reminds us of the solemn truth that we proclaim what we really are by the way we react when trouble and affliction tests us. In many ways it is the best test of all for it shows exactly where we stand.

When you hear a pastor preach it is easy to think – even if it is not said – that they know little about affliction. Most pastors have a deep knowledge of such matters; things that most of their congregations will know nothing about. These trials and afflictions can be their own, those of their loved ones; and those in the church and wider community. Martin Luther doubtless had this in view when he said, 'Three things make a minister; prayer, temptation, and affliction.'

A true believer then can sink into bitterness, and this too is a very dangerous condition to be in: which is why verse fifteen warns us against it so seriously. Just as one poisonous root can infect a whole crop, one embittered person in a church can cause great damage to the whole fellowship. Bad attitudes are contagious and can rapidly spread to others. It is amazing how susceptible we all are to these noxious influences, but we are – because of sin and the Fall. We would do well to remember that just as a spirit of joy and unity can affect a whole congregation, so too can a spirit of bitterness and resentment. God keep us from it! Rather, may '...much grace be upon us all' (Acts 4:33).

These are three of the most common manifestations of a faulty response to discipline, and so long as we continue to react in such ways, so long we will fail to learn the lessons our Father is endeavouring to teach us.

> Quiet, Lord, my forward heart;
> Make me teachable and mild...
> *John Newton*

But having looked at the *wrong* ways of responding to discipline, we turn now to the *right* way.

RESPONDING CORRECTLY TO DISCIPLINE

Obviously, a *right* response will be the exact *opposite* to those three ways we have looked at that are wrong. There are two *positive* aspects referred to in this passage.

1. To realize the purpose of trouble and affliction

'Endure hardship as discipline...' (or son-training), says this man. We have already established that Christians do suffer hardship in this life – and in some cases, extreme hardship. So when we are in that position, and going through a season of unusual buffetings, how can we 'keep on keeping on' – and do so not in a spirit of depression, but rejoicing? (James 1:2). To put it in Paul's triumphant words at the end of Romans chapter 8, how can we be more than conquerors (literally, *hyper*-conquerors), when all these things seem to be conspiring against us, 'to drive us to despair'? There is only one answer; we need to grasp the divine purpose and rationale in it all – that everything that happens to us is all part of this great training programme through which God is putting his children. Hardship, whatever form it takes, is never because of 'bad luck' – neither is it ever accidental or meaningless.

Prepare us for Glory

Instead, the suffering and unhappiness we experience is sent with this great end in view – to prepare us for glory! As John Trapp, the old Puritan commentator, put it, somewhat quaintly, 'God has only one Son without sin, but none without sorrow.' So in all this, we can say with Richard Baxter:

> Christ leads me through no darker rooms
> Than he went through before.

We are simply following in his steps. Think of it in medical terms. Someone is taken seriously ill, but the treatment prescribed is very painful. As a result, the person *feels* worse than ever, and is tempted to discharge themself. But if the doctor is able to assure them that the treatment is going to really help and effect a cure, then that changes their whole attitude. Not only are they willing to endure the treatment, no matter how great the discomfort, but if they know it is doing them good, they begins to feel better already! It is the same in the realm of the spirit. John Newton expressed it perfectly in a well-known hymn:

> Since all that I meet
> Shall work for my good,
> The bitter is sweet,
> The medicine is food;
> Though painful at present,
> 'Twill cease before long;
> And then, O how pleasant
> The conqueror's song!

2. We must also submit to the one who lays the trials on us.

We are to look beyond mere second causes to the great original and uncaused cause, our loving, eternal, heavenly Father himself. We need to realize that he is infinitely more concerned about us and our eternal welfare than we are ourselves. So verse nine urges us to 'submit to the Father of our spirits...and live!' We respected our earthly parents who disciplined us (or we should have done). How much more should we respect our heavenly Father whose discipline is never unkind or too severe. The argument is irrefutable and again we see how the Scripture reasons with us.

But we need that! How slow we are to yield and surrender ourselves to our Father's dealings with us! How quick to grumble and complain! That was one of the great failings of the Children of Israel in the wilderness. They were continually murmuring and complaining against Moses – or even against God – and usually both!

Measured out

Are we submitting to God or are we murmuring against him? That does not mean to submit sullenly, as children do sometimes because they have no choice. Are we subjecting ourselves gladly and willingly? Are we clear that every trial that comes our way is measured out in perfect wisdom and in deepest love? We would all admit in theory that a complaining spirit is sinful, but many no doubt, would limit it to that of very minor sins. If so, we are wrong!

Our greatest need then is the grace of humility. As the Apostle Peter put it to a people who, like the Hebrews, were suffering persecution, 'Humble yourselves, therefore, under God's mighty hand, that he may lift you up in due time. Cast all your anxiety on him because he cares for you.' (1 Peter 5:6-7). Seek the grace of patience, or 'Christian resignation', as it used to be called; and say with the Psalmist, 'I know, O Lord, that your laws are righteous, and in faithfulness you have afflicted me.' (Psalm 119:75).

> Trials must and will befall;
> But with humble faith we see
> Love inscribed upon them all,
> This is happiness to me.
> *William Cowper, Olney Hymns, Book III, No. 16*

RESPONDING PROFITABLY TO DISCIPLINE

We need to notice very carefully a phrase, which appears at the end of verse eleven. 'No discipline seems pleasant at the time, but painful. Later on, however, it produces a harvest of righteousness and peace for *those who have been trained by it.*' The whole intention and purpose of discipline is to produce a spiritual harvest in the life of the believer concerned. But discipline does not have that effect automatically. That goal is only brought to fruition in those who have been trained by it. It does not just happen.

The fact that we are being disciplined, and are suffering hardship, is no guarantee that it will lead to this harvest of the fruit of the Spirit. The real issue is this: how am I reacting to the training schedule? Tragically, in many instances, it has driven a person from God and hardened their hearts still further against him. It has had the opposite effect to what it ought to have had and has driven people away from God, not to him.

Therefore, we need to earnestly pray that God would sanctify our troubles to us, and enable us to rightly profit from them. When we do truly submit to him, this is what follows: 'How much more we should submit to the Father of our spirits and live.' *Live!* – with all that the Scripture pours into that word: of abounding spiritual life in *this* world, and everlasting life in the world to come! When we submit truly to God's discipline, this will be the outcome – *life* – with all that goes with it; of peace and joy, happiness and assurance.

By contrast, refusal to submit brings about the exact opposite – *death,* and all that goes with that.

Let us thank God for the teaching; thank him for sending his beloved Son to save us; thank him that having begun a good work in us, he will most certainly carry it on, and complete it when that glorious day dawns, and the shadows of this earthly life flee away.

'Grant, Almighty God, that as thou at this day mercifully sparest us, when yet in various ways we provoke thy displeasure, - O grant, that we may not harden ourselves against thy chastisements, but that thy forbearance may lead us to repentance, and that also thy scourges may do us good, and that we may so truly turn to thee, that our whole life may testify that we are in our hearts changed...'

Prayer of John Calvin, following his Twelfth Lecture on Jeremiah

chastisement – human and divine

Endure hardship as discipline; God is treating you as sons. For what son is not disciplined by his father? If you are not disciplined (and everyone undergoes discipline), then you are illegitimate children and not true sons. Moreover, we have all had human fathers who disciplined us and we respected them for it. How much more should we submit to the Father of our spirits and live! Our fathers disciplined us for a little while as they thought best; but God disciplines us for our good, that we may share in his holiness.'

Hebrews 12:7-10

The purpose for which this letter was sent was a pastoral one. The author was extremely concerned about the people to whom he was writing. They were passing through a season of great trial and affliction, and unless we are alert in a spiritual sense, such times invariably lead to discouragement, even depression, in the Christian life. That in turn often leads to backsliding, with its fearful tendency to complete apostasy from the faith; hence this man's anxiety about the recipients of his epistle who were clearly in great danger of this terrible end.

False reading

The reason why these people were so downhearted by their troubles, which were real enough, was because they had

completely misinterpreted God's dealings with them in this situation. As Philip Hughes puts it in his commentary at this point:
'The discouragement of the recipients of this letter is attribu-
table…to a false reading of the situation in which they find themselves. Such hardship and affliction as they have had to endure
in consequence of their Christian profession does not mean, as
some seem to have assumed, that God is unconcerned about
their welfare, and has left them without his aid and support.'[1]

That is not the position at all; on the contrary! Far from
neglecting them, God has been dealing with them, demonstrating that he has their best interests at heart by treating them as
good fathers always will treat their children – they will discipline
and train them.

There is nothing more practically relevant and up to date
than the teaching before us. That is brought out in a striking
way by the tense used in verse five: 'And you have forgotten
that word of encouragement that addresses you as sons…' So
although what follows is a quotation from a passage of Scripture written a thousand years earlier – by King Solomon – it
does *not* say, 'that *addressed* you as sons' (past tense), but rather,
'that *addresses* you as sons!'

The Living Word

The inference is clear. The utterance of Scripture is referred to
as the very word of God, speaking to his children directly in
their present circumstances and situation. Moreover, that word
is spoken immediately to every age and generation. Another
example of this same principle is in the sevenfold exhortation
found in the second and third chapters of the book of Revelation – 'He who has an ear, let him hear what the Spirit says to
the churches.' It is what the Spirit *says*, not *said!* This Book is
not a dead letter, locked up in history. It is the Living Word of
the Living God, the voice from heaven which speaks to us and
to our contemporary situation as really, and as directly, as it did
to the people of Solomon's day who first heard it. Here is

existential pastoral theology in the truest sense of the word. Having this, what further need is there of any extra-Scriptural 'word from the Lord' to instruct and comfort us in our trials?

A Perennial Problem

The issue here is the whole problem of suffering, especially suffering in the lives of those who do believe in God. The people to whom this letter was originally addressed were in difficulties for this very reason – that to them, what they were enduring did not tally with their concept of the Gospel, 'the Good News'.

Many people have expressed their sense of disappointment with the Christian message because for them it has not done what they expected it to do. There have been thousands of people in Britain alone who have defected from the ranks of organized religion since World War II. If it were possible to have taken up a census we would find that a considerable proportion had left the church for this very reason – that they had experienced sufferings and troubles to a degree which, in their own minds at least, they could not reconcile with the love of God.

This has been particularly so in the case of those who have been prematurely bereaved as the result of war. They just cannot harmonize the love of God with the terrible things that are happening in the world – and in many instances, to them personally. Many have lost sons – young men of fine and noble character who went, either to fight for their country, or to fight against oppression in various places around the world, and never returned from the battlefield. They see this happening to their loved ones while others living evil and unworthy lives, are allowed to live, and subsequently to prosper and be successful. The consequence is that many then turned their backs on the church.

Makes you wonder

There was a programme on UK television during which veterans recounted their wartime experiences, and spoke of the lifelong stress that many of them endured subsequently. One old soldier said this: 'It makes you wonder how a God of love could have allowed it.' Such instances could be multiplied. But this whole problem is a much wider one than that posed by sufferings related to times of war. Many who have tried to live a godly life but have found themsleves overwhelmed by financial problems and difficulties – even to the point of bankruptcy. By contrast the wicked and ungodly person often seems to flourish like 'a green bay tree', as the psalmist puts it. Then there are those who suffer constant ill-health or disability, while still others experience the tragic and heart-rending loss of a loved one: when someone near and dear to them is taken at an early age – maybe through some dreadful accident. As a result many men and women come to the conclusion that such troubles are utterly inconsistent with the Christian message and its promises.

I was speaking to a neighbour whose husband had died: she said, 'It makes you wonder…' The implication, though unspoken, was nevertheless quite plain and clear. However, there are others who, although they too feel confused and unhappy, nevertheless do retain allegiance to the church. They do not understand why God should permit their suffering, and are quite unable to engage in *theodicy* – justification of the ways of God – but they stay in the church out of sheer *loyalty*; and maybe habit. It is to such that the writer to the Hebrews speaks particularly. There is no point in denying that the harsh realities of life in this world can appear to contradict the glorious promises of the Gospel. But there is a scriptural rationale for the ways of God, and the apparent inconsistency between his promises and his providence, as we see from this passage.

A COMPARISON

It is a comparison between an *earthly* father and the *heavenly* Father in the way they treat their children. This is the emphasis in verses seven to nine. 'Before we go any further,' says this writer in effect, 'we all recognize the fact that earthly parents seek to discipline and train their offspring.' Their great concern is to prepare and fit them for life, and bring them to moral and physical maturity. 'All right,' he says, 'we all accept that at the *natural* level. That is common ground. But exactly the same principle applies in the realm of the *spiritual*, in our relationship to our Father in heaven.' 'There should not be any problem over this,' he says. In other words, the writer to the Hebrews is using what we call an *ad hominem* argument to make his point: he is appealing to a practice which humanly speaking, is accepted by common consent.

Anyone who gives thought to this must agree that training and discipline is not the mark of a harsh and uncaring parent. Rather, it is the mark of a father who is deeply and lovingly concerned for his child, and has their well-being in mind. 'Well then,' says this man, 'work out the implication for yourselves. If this is so with an *earthly* father, how much more true it must be of our *heavenly* Father!'

Expect this

Admittedly, we are living in such soft, undisciplined days that we can scarcely use the argument from analogy, as this man does. Yet for all the failure to discipline that is so true of the modern generation, even the weakest and most remiss parent can see the force of the argument. Just as *earthly* parents worthy of the name will discipline their children (albeit badly and inconsistently), so too will our *heavenly* parent discipline his children (with perfect discipline). We can expect this, says the writer to the Hebrews; it goes with the relationship.

Discipline (and the chastisement this sometimes requires), may be very hurtful and hard to bear at times, but it is nonetheless necessary, and the good parent will not neglect it. God carries out this disciplinary process quite deliberately, as a vital part of our sanctification. Because that is so, we need to examine ourselves, and to ask questions: 'Am I aware of this? Am I conscious of being dealt with?' If we are not aware of a training process, it seems doubtful whether we belong to the family of God at all! We are more likely to be spiritually illegitimate – a false convert! '…The Lord disciplines those he loves…' – that is a fundamental principle, admitting of no exceptions.

The person who ought to feel unhappy – indeed alarmed – is not the one who is acutely *conscious* of discipline, but the one who is not even remotely aware of it. Far from being upset and resentful at discipline, we ought to thank God for it, and be grateful that he perseveres with us at all, because that is the best proof that we are true children. John Trapp, the old Puritan, put it pithily: 'Corrections are pledges of our adoption and badges of our sonship…As God corrects none but his own, so all that *are* his shall be sure to have it.'

Why?

So often people turn to the Bible as if it were a pocket calculator which gives a detailed explanation and answer to every trial that confronts us. When fine Christians are tragically bereaved while still young, some will want to know why – as if the New Testament has an immediate answer to the problem. But it never claims to do that, which is why these people are so disappointed, because they had always assumed that it did. Nowhere does the Bible promise us detailed and precise answers to all our problems. Instead, it lays down these general principles; such as we have here.

This may seem strange to modern ears, which want instant answers and direct comfort. But that is not the Biblical way. The approach here is always deductive: it reasons with us, but it does so on the basis of doctrine – in this case the doctrine of sonship.

Magic circle

Christians are not promised charmed or magical lives. It is a strange fact that somehow many otherwise sensible believers have picked up the notion that once a person is converted, he or she automatically lives 'happily ever after'. That belongs more to the realm of Hans Anderson's fairy tales than the Bible. Many people seem to imagine that as Christians, they have stepped into a kind of magic circle in which, although *others* are allowed to suffer, *they* are miraculously protected. It sounds wonderful! The trouble is, it is not true. If anything, it is the exact opposite. True Christians, simply because they have a heavenly Father who is training them for glory, can *expect* to be disciplined. In John Calvin's words, 'There is nothing more to be dreaded than that the Lord should allow us loose reins.' No doubt more detailed explanations will be given to us when we reach the better world to come, especially as to why we suffer in particular ways.

An accident caused the death of a pastor's son, just shortly before he was due to leave on missionary service overseas. He left behind a wife and baby daughter. A fellow pastor made the comment: 'In this life, God owes us no explanations.'

Commenting on this passage in Hebrews, John Owen writes: 'They deceive themselves who expect to be in God's family, and not to be under his chastening discipline.' That being so, may God enable us to say (and to sing!)

> Whatever my lot, Thou hast taught me to say,
> It is well, it is well with my soul.
> *Horatio G. Spafford*

This wonderful hymn was written after Spafford's four daughters were drowned in a mid-Atlantic shipping accident. Only his wife Anna survived. Again we can repeat the quote: 'In this life, God owes us no explanations.'

A CONTRAST

We see this from the 'but' of verse ten. What is *common* both to earthly fathers and our heavenly Father, is that they discipline their children. But there the similarity ends and now the writer to the Hebrews brings out the *differences*. There are two distinctive characteristics of the discipline administered by our *heavenly* parent that mark it off from that meted out by an *earthly* parent.

1. Discipline administered by our heavenly Father is *long-term*

It takes the long view in a way that human discipline does not. 'Our fathers disciplined us for *a little while…*' which means that the training given by earthly parents to their children is concerned with *this* life; and even then, only while the child is growing up. Once they 'fly the nest', they have to discipline themselves.

By contrast, God's discipline always has our final well-being in mind, and is dispensed in the light of eternity. As D.L.Moody expressed it, 'The rough hewing of reproof is only to square us for the heavenly building.'

The trouble with many, who have experienced some great trial or other, is that they tend to think only in terms of *this* life. As they look ahead to ten, twenty, thirty years of suffering they wonder how they can bear the burden for so long – and do not look beyond that. But God always *does*, and as his discipline looks 'beyond the veil', so his training regime is carried out with that in view.

That is not the only difference between *earthly* and *heavenly* discipline. Another feature that differentiates the two is that:

2. God's discipline is always applied in *perfect love*, and in *perfect wisdom*.

This is not true of us, not even of the kindest of earthly parents. 'Our fathers disciplined us for a little while as they thought *best*', says this man, or 'as they saw *fit*'. But as those who are parents know only too well, our children are not slow to point out how inconsistent we often are, how fallible! What parent can put his hand on his heart and claim that in the exercise of discipline, he, or she, has never lost their temper? How easily we get frayed at the edges, how capricious we can be, no matter how unintentionally.

Probably we have all had the experience of being in a supermarket and witnessing what happens when a child is obstreperous, and the stressed mother loses her patience! The child gets a hard slap given in temper, which is *not* the way to do it! Even the most worthy parents can be motivated by the irritation of the moment, rather than a genuine concern for the good of the child and to implement discipline that is fair and appropriate to the misdemeanour concerned.

But God never just reacts and lashes out. As Calvin says, 'There is nothing in God's discipline that is out of control.' As our text puts it, '...God disciplines us for our good.' Our Father's discipline is always carried out in the infallible knowledge of what we need, of the particular circumstances in which we are placed, and also of what we are able to bear – by his grace. He always 'tempers the wind to the shorn lamb'. To quote John Trapp again, 'It is in mercy and in measure that God chastiseth his children.'

A great principle

We are now in a position to see a great principle of pastoral theology which the author of Hebrews is setting before us. Knowing that his readers were confused about God's dealings with them, he tells them to start with that of which they were certain – the great over-arching fact of which every Christian is sure – that God is love. Incidentally, that is the true scientific method always. Instead of jumping to unwarranted conclusions, putting up a theory and assuming it to be a fact, the true scientist will always start from the known, and then, but not till then, proceed to the unknown.

Rock of Ages

The writer here is telling us to follow exactly the same method when confronted by problems in the Christian life. You start with what you know to be true. Plant your feet on the Rock of Ages, and say to yourself: 'There are many things I do not understand; things which baffle and mystify the intellect, but this I do know: my heavenly Father loves me so much and is so concerned about my eternal future in the glory, that he sent his own dear Son to this evil world, and even to the cross, for my sake. So whatever is happening to me of this I am certain, and I take my stand on it. After all, if he went to the extremity of handing over his Son to such unimaginable suffering in my place, then whatever he allows to happen to me in this world, must be for my good.' So, as a wise man by the name of Lord Bacon once put it, 'Let not the things you are uncertain of, rob you of that of which you are certain.'

Is not the trouble with us that we want to enter the great University of Heaven without going through the Training School of this life, and the discipline and tests which this involves? Changing the illustration a little, we would all like to skip GCSEs and 'A' levels, and get into University without entering the examination halls at all! But it cannot be done. We ought to thank God for that, because he really does know what is best for us. As Thomas Brooks puts it: 'God's corrections are our instructions, his lashes our lessons, his scourges our schoolmasters'[2].

A CONCERN

'God disciplines us for our good, that (in order that, with a view towards) we may share in his holiness' (verse ten).

Here, we are taken another step on in this man's reasoning. If we grasp the teaching here it will be a giant step forward in our understanding of God's dealings with his children. The teaching is this: as our heavenly Father, God is much more concerned about our *holiness* than about our *happiness!* With us, it tends to be the other way round, does it not? The criterion we apply to life is, 'Does it make me happy?' We want to have everything our own way – just like children. So immediately something happens to us that is unpleasant and painful, and which makes us unhappy, we begin to doubt the love of God. We are like the boy who thinks his father is being unfair to him in not allowing him to do what other boys do. Other parents allow their children to stay out late, and do not insist that they do their homework. In his foolishness, he wishes his parents were easygoing too. Such a boy does not understand what is best for him. The question is, do *we?*

Like him

What *is* best for us? Our first and greatest need always is to know God, and be like him – to 'be holy as he is holy' (1 Peter 1:15-16). This is essential, for as verse fourteen reminds us, 'without holiness no one will see the Lord.' According to Thomas Brooks, the Puritan, holiness is 'the crown and glory of Christianity'. Without holiness, there will be no beatific vision. But that is what we are being prepared for. And when we do see him with unclouded sight, we shall then see clearly the loving hand of God in all our trials.

May God enable us to say with the hymn writer:

I thank Thee more, that all our joy
Is touched with pain,
That shadows fall on brightest hours,
That thorns remain;
So that earth's bliss may be our guide,
And not our chain.

Adelaide Anne Procter

harvest time

'…God disciplines us for our good, that we may share in his holiness. No discipline seems pleasant at the time, but painful. Later on, however, it produces a harvest of righteousness and peace for those who have been trained by it.'

Hebrews 12:10b-11

In previous chapters we have established that this letter was written to Hebrew Christians who were suffering intense persecution for Christ's sake – particularly from their unbelieving fellow Hebrews. As a result they were not only greatly discouraged but many were wondering whether, by casting their lot in with Jesus as the promised Messiah, they had not committed a monumental mistake for which they were now suffering. At such times, the temptation is to feel that God is displeased with us – even *against* us. If he is not, then why are we having such a hard time? Does God not care? In such situations, the problem can appear insoluble.

There is an answer, and it is provided in this wonderful teaching on son-training. Far from God being against them, or unconcerned about their welfare, the trials these people were enduring really meant the exact opposite! It showed that he was a true Father, by treating them as good fathers always will treat their sons. They will train and discipline them. As the archetypal Father, God is no exception to that rule. Indeed, he sets the standard in this respect, and always has our ultimate good in view.

As we see from verses five and six, the writer's method is to reason with us from Scripture. Our heavenly Father pays us the compliment of treating us as adults. He explains why we need discipline, and argues out his case with us. We see how Scripture reasons with us on the basis of how we deal with our children, at the human level. Follow out the logic of that, and we will realize why our heavenly Father disciplines us.

To grasp this important principle is a mark of maturity and growth in grace. The Psalmist understood this as we see from his reiterated comments in Psalm 119. 'Before I was afflicted I went astray, but now I obey your word...It was good for me to be afflicted so that I might learn your decrees...I know, O Lord, that your laws are righteous, and in faithfulness you have afflicted me' (verses 67, 71 & 75). Here is a man who has profited from his troubles, and learned his lesson, albeit the hard way.

In the words of Henry Law, '...Despise not the scourge. It has a teaching voice. It is held by a loving Father's hand.'

THE PAIN OF CHASTISEMENT

'No discipline seems pleasant at the time, but painful...' This is not to imply that the hurt caused by affliction is only *apparent*, and not real. Unlike some of the cults, such as *Christian Science* (so-called), the Bible is always realistic, and never denies, or even plays down, the reality of pain, whether to the feelings or the body.

If you tell someone who is in deep distress that their pain or anguish is not nearly as bad as they are making out, that will only exacerbate the problem by creating an additional cause of annoyance! The writer to the Hebrews is by no means trying to depreciate the hurt and suffering his readers have experienced. He is facing it in all its misery and heartache. But do not stop there – take the long view, and this is what follows: 'Later on, however, it produces a harvest!' Never lose sight of the 'later on'!

However, that is *future*, but what about the pain of discipline in the *present*. There is no way of avoiding this. In the words of

C.H. Spurgeon, 'The sword of *justice* no longer threatens us, but the rod of parental *correction* is still in use.' The whole point of 'the rod' is to cause us pain. In a world like this, and with a fallen nature that carries with it such propensities for evil, the Christian can never expect to be free from discipline.

Passing strange

The Apostle Peter puts it in a similar way to his readers, who were in an almost identical situation to that of the Hebrews. 'Dear friends, do not be surprised at the painful trial you are suffering, as though something strange were happening to you.' (1 Peter 4:12). But like these Hebrews, and no doubt like some of us, they were surprised. They thought it passing strange that God should allow them to suffer.

Why should we not be surprised? Because of who we are, and whom we follow. As Martin Luther put it, 'If Christ wore a crown of *thorns*, why should his followers expect only a crown of *roses*?' Because there is so much remaining corruption and unworthiness about us, we always *need* discipline. Thomas Brooks puts it quaintly, but nonetheless effectively, in a typical Puritan aphorism: 'God would not rub so hard, were it not to fetch out the dirt and spots that be in his people.' This ought to be self-evident, but how easily we forget it. So often, all we are aware of is the *pain* of discipline, not the *need* of it, or the long-term *intention* behind it.

Short-sighted

One of the greatest effects of sin is to make us spiritually short-sighted. Consequently, we invariably tend to view affliction only in the light of the painful *present*, and not in view of a *future* benefit. To give a simple illustration: if one is going round an art gallery, and looking at old masters, the way to view some works from the best advantage is to step back a little. It is rather like that in the Christian life. So often, we are unable to 'see the wood for the trees': unable to view the larger picture.

Many Christians can look back on painful episodes in their lives which at the time caused much hurt and anguish, but for which now, standing back as it were, they can thank God. A perfect example of this is seen in the life of Jacob. He had lost Joseph, as he thought, and the point came when it seemed as if he had lost Simeon too. In his agony, he just cried out, 'Everything is *against* me!' (Gen. 42:36). But it was not. Later on Jacob discovered his mistake, and found that in reality all those events were *for* him and had been working together for good, both for him and his beloved family.

Chastisement is intended to be painful, because only in that way will it produce the desired effect. It is the same with our children. If when they needed the firm hand of correction, we simply gave them a treat, what signal would that be sending? The punishment is sent in love, for as C.H. Spurgeon put it, 'chastisement is blended with tenderness', but it *hurts* nevertheless.

If you are God's child, he is absolutely committed to preparing you for glory. When, in his infinite wisdom, this involves painful trials, it is always with that great end in view.

Spiritual lessons

The trial can be almost anything – a great disappointment in life, or someone letting you down badly. It may be some financial loss, a change for the worse in your material circumstances. It may be that God allows you to make a mistake in your life, the consequences of which are irreversible. Perhaps your health will suffer, or that of someone near and dear to you; there may be an accident, a calamity, death – the Bible is full of such incidents. It may even be ill-treatment at the hands of a fellow-Christian; there is nothing more hurtful. George Whitefield once said that he expected the contradiction of *sinners* – it was the contradiction of *saints* he found so hard to bear! These things happen – no child of God is ever exempt from the slings and arrows of adversity.

However dark and mysterious are the troubles of this life, we must never forget that they are always less than our sins deserve; and rightly received they are replete with spiritual lessons. These things are not only useful, but absolutely necessary for us. God *could* sanctify us without trials, but the fact is that he has not chosen to do so, and we must submit to that. Besides that, as the Bible makes crystal clear, there is no situation in which we can glorify God more, than in the fire of affliction.

In the year 1552, five young students who belonged to the new Église Reformée in France, were imprisoned for their faith and then cruelly martyred. Whilst in prison, they wrote to the Church in Geneva (where Calvin was) as follows: 'We testify that this is the true school of the children of God, in which they learn more than the disciples of the philosophers ever did in their universities.' They then praised God for giving them by his grace 'not only the *theory* of his Word, but also the *practice* of it.'[1] May we know the like experience!

THE PURPOSE OF CHASTISEMENT

Our heavenly Father never chastises his children for the sake of it: there is always an end in view. But what does it do for us: how does it help us? Rightly understood this teaching on discipline is one of the most comforting truths in the entire Bible. My only hope of arriving safely in glory is the fact that the whole of my salvation is in God's hands. 'Salvation is of the Lord!' (Jonah 2:9 KJV). Every part of it is of him. This is entirely his work, and therefore I can be sure that if I am a child of his, he will complete the work that he has begun in me (cf. Phil. 1:6). If God has put his mighty hand of grace upon me, then he will continue to deal with me until that glorious goal is realized.

And yet we have to add this: if a Christian grows slack and careless, and fails to implement in his life the positive teaching of Scripture, then God has many *other means* he can use in order to bring him to that goal. This is an awesome, almost frightening thought. At the same time it is wonderfully reassuring that if you belong to him, then he will do anything to perfect you, because his covenant love has guaranteed to get you to glory. But from time to time that may require stern measures.

Archibald Alexander of Old Princeton wrote as follows in a letter to a recently bereaved widower, 'Alas! when we are at ease, and living in prosperity, how cold and careless are we in our devotional exercises! Engrossed with worldly business, and too well satisfied with creature comforts, we forget God, and lose sight of heaven. From this state of alienation we are seldom reclaimed by the Word alone. Indeed, in such a frame, the truth can scarcely be said to have access to our minds. But when the severe stroke of our Father's rod is experienced, we begin to feel with keen sensibility, and to pray with unwonted fervency and importunity. And the afflicted child of God thus arrested, convinced and humbled, cannot rest until he obtains some new evidence of reconciliation, some manifestation of the love and favour of his offended Father.'[2]

Slowness to learn

We so often fall back into living as if this was the only life and the only world. We have to be weaned from this way of thinking – and only God can do it. But such is our recalcitrance and our slowness to learn, that as Alexander's remarks make clear, God has to take us in hand, and 'turn the sound up', so that we have to listen. This world is not our home. It is more like the porch to a great mansion where we take off our muddy shoes before being allowed to enter. If only we could view life consistently in that way, it would transform our whole attitude (and at the same time solve most of our problems).

Therefore in chastisement, God is teaching us the better way. So, as Matthew Henry puts it: 'When we are chastened, we must *pray to be taught*...It is not the chastening itself that does good, but the teaching that goes along with it, and is the exposition of it.'

The need of holiness

In verse ten we are told that the whole end and aim of discipline is that we might share in God's holiness. The term *holiness* occurs some nine hundred times in the Scriptures, which gives some indication of the supreme importance the Word of God attaches to this issue. What does the Bible *mean* by holiness? It is a profound yet very simple concept, though it is also something that has been greatly misunderstood. Holiness does *not* mean a Pharisaical list of do's and don'ts, and it certainly does not mean a haughty superiority, which draws up the skirts of its own supposed righteousness and despises others who do not share its shibboleths. In its original meaning, holiness does not even signify purity, although that is an implication of holiness. Rather, holiness means to be 'set apart from common or ordinary use, for the purpose of being devoted to God'.

That essential and basic meaning can be further considered under its negative and positive aspects. From the *negative* standpoint, holiness means to be set apart *from* sin and defilement. From the *positive* aspect, it means to be set apart *to* God and righteousness. In practice then, holiness means separation from sin, and consecration to God and his service. Even the vessels and furniture in the Tabernacle and the Temple were described as 'holy', because they were set apart from secular use, and used solely in connection with the service of God.

The really amazing thing is that we are called to be sharers in the very holiness of God himself! In the words of the Apostle Peter, 'As he who called you is holy, so be holy in all you do; for it is written: "Be holy, because I am holy."' (1 Peter 1:15). Maybe we are wondering how we can possibly be said to be holy as God is holy. Is it even conceivable?

No doubt there is a final mystery here which we can never fathom in this life. But this much is certain: there is a way in which the holiness or separateness of God is unique and cannot possibly be shared with his creatures. In this sense it refers to the divine transcendence – that God is 'a cut above' the whole of created reality, dwelling in light which is unapproachable.

New creation

But, there is another sense in which the holiness of God is

communicable to man, by virtue of the new birth and by which we are made to 'participate in the divine nature' (2 Peter 1:4). God's aim for all his chosen people is to separate them from sin and this 'present evil age' (Galatians 1:4), and 'to purify for himself a people that are his very own' (Titus 2:14). What is the *chief end* of the Christian life? It is not only to *know* God, but also to become *like* him. This Biblical definition of a Christian is almost beyond our conception. They are people in whom the divine character is formed. Not only are their sins forgiven; they are nothing less than a *new creation,* in whom the very nature and traits of God himself are being formed. What a marvel this is!

The whole aim and object of God's disciplinary dealings with his children is to make them more like himself. Furthermore, this is an ongoing and developing process in this world. Are *you* 'making every effort...to be holy'? (verse 14). Philip Hughes puts it searchingly in these words: 'How easily the desire for holiness is set aside when our worldly affairs are proceeding comfortably!' He adds, '...how needful then, is God's fatherly discipline.'

Our desires after holiness are so weak, and so sporadic; it is almost as if we fear the loss of personal freedom. Spurgeon has a word for us: 'A liberty to be holy is a grander liberty than a license to be sinful...a liberty to trample upon conquered lusts, this is an infinitely wider liberty than that which would permit me to be the comfortable slave of sin, and yet indulge the delusive hope that I may one day enter the kingdom of heaven.'[3]

To use a simple illustration: we need only ask when a railway locomotive is most free? Is it when running on the rails for which it was made? Or is it when it jumps the rails and leaves the track marked out for it? The answer is self evident!

We must ask ourselves if the discipline we are experiencing is having its divinely intended effect? Here is a simple test. Is there a harvest coming to fruition in my life? Is there fruit to be seen, especially the fruit of *righteousness* and *peace*? Why does the horticulturist prune and cut back so rigorously? He does so to make the tree even more fruitful (cf. John 15:2).

Righteousness

Why does God want us to produce righteousness? The answer is found in the very meaning of the word. *Right*eousness means just what it says: that which is truly right (in God's eyes) and in accordance with the only true standard, the righteous law of God expressed in the Ten Commandments, and the spiritual exposition of it in the Sermon on the Mount. The mark of a true believer is that he is not satisfied with being forgiven, wonderful though that is. His greatest desire is increasing likeness to God, conformity of heart and life to the revealed will of God in Scripture. He 'hungers and thirsts for righteousness' (Matt. 5:6). Do we know something of that? Does it grieve us that we make so little progress in that direction? 'If you love me, keep my commandments', said our Lord to his disciples. It is a vital test of our position.

Peace

Peace is another great Biblical word. Here, the King James Version (AV) is a preferable rendering: 'nevertheless…it yieldeth the peaceable fruit of righteousness.' So there are not two fruits being referred to, but one. It is the fruit of righteousness, and yet a righteousness that is characterized by peace. As with the righteousness of God, it is a *peaceable* righteousness.

Why is this righteousness described as 'peaceable'? Because there is a type of righteousness (so-called), which is hard and unloving, and not at all peaceable. It is a righteousness which is legalistic and censorious; a righteousness which is proud and unbending – and as such is the very opposite of God. He is the righteous God, yes – but he is also the Saviour, 'the God of peace' (Hebrews 13:20).

The question for us is this: are we like that? Are we peaceable in our reactions to others, or do we easily flare up in self-righteous anger? The peaceable man is a man who controls his tongue for the sake of peace. Sometimes one hears even Christians say, 'I am going to give him (or her) a piece of my mind!' But what if we all did that? The trouble with most of us is that we tend to take things personally: we are over-sensitive to criticism and imagined slights and react accordingly. But that is the way of war, not peace. That is *self.* Instead, we have to humble ourselves, be ready to apologize, and seek always to be friendly and approachable – as God is with us.

In the words of verse fourteen we are to 'make every effort to live in peace with all men.' James puts it perfectly, '...the wisdom that comes from heaven is first of all pure, then peace-loving, considerate, submissive, full of mercy and good fruit, impartial and sincere. Peacemakers who sow in peace raise a harvest of righteousness.' (3:17,18). The whole purpose of God's disciplinary procedure is to produce that kind of harvest in our lives. Is it doing so with us?

A Prerequisite

But no harvest of any kind ever just appears automatically. If the farmer wants to harvest an abundant crop in the autumn, he needs to put in a great deal of work earlier on in the year. In a word, there is a prerequisite to all this. We are told that the discipline through which our heavenly Father puts us, only produces a harvest in the lives of those who have been *trained* by it. Maybe I am aware of the chastening hand of God in my life, and the experience may be a very painful one. But hardship and affliction in and of themselves will never produce the fruit of peaceable righteousness. How am I responding to chastisement and discipline? Am I being *trained* by it? Many a person has been corrected by God, maybe severely, but has not profited from the experience – has not learned the lesson – and has gone on in the old same way. Rather, we need to consider our ways, and having examined ourselves, to plead with the Holy Spirit to enable us to truly submit to the discipline, and profit from it. Above all, we need to turn to our Lord and Saviour Jesus Christ, in renewed penitence and faith. He it is, who in perfect righteousness has made peace, 'through his blood, shed on the cross' (Colossians 1:20).

a spiritual work-out

'Therefore, strengthen your feeble arms and weak knees! "Make level paths for your feet," so that the lame may not be disabled, but rather healed.'

Hebrews 12:12-13

Throughout the studies in this passage of Scripture, it has been important to keep in mind the context in which it was written. Many of these people were cast down and discouraged in their Christian lives mainly because they had completely misunderstood God's dealings with them in that situation. He deals with us as good fathers always will deal with their children – they will not allow them to have too soft and easy a time of it. Instead, they will discipline and train them – even chastise them when that is required.

Because God is not only our Father, but is absolutely sovereign in the affairs of men, it is no problem for him to direct all the troubles and trials of life and cause them to work for good and the well-being of our souls. Fred Mitchell, once Director of the former China Inland Mission, put it perfectly: 'the heavenly Father has no spoiled children. He loves them too much to allow that.' There is no mystery in the fact that these Hebrews were going through a hard time. They were suffering these things not so much *in spite* of being children of God, but *because* they were!

The Scriptures emphasize constantly that we all *need* God to deal with us in this way. A moment's thought should be enough to see why. The fact that we have been converted and become Christians does not mean that we have arrived; that we are perfect. There are certain things about us that need to be dealt with – certain angularities – and God often uses trying circumstances to teach us lessons it seems we could not have learned in any other way. So long as we are in this world, there will be dangers and temptations that are a threat to our spiritual life, and we need to be protected from them. On the other hand, if we have fallen prey to these enemies that 'war against your soul' (1 Peter 2:11), we need to be restored – and that again is why God chastises us.

Pride – no greater folly

There are so many wrongful tendencies in our lives that need to be dealt with that space forbids any attempt at exhaustive treatment, even if that were possible. But there are certain more obvious things for which our heavenly Father has to take us in hand. The main one surely is pride: self-reliance – the feeling almost that we can go it alone and 'paddle our own canoe'. There is no greater folly, and yet because we are 'born in sin', this fearful tendency frequently reasserts itself. Spiritual pride is such a terrible danger to our souls, that even if we have not succumbed to it in any particular way, God will allow things to happen in our lives as a means of *preventing* us from falling – as a kind of spiritual prophylactic. In the second letter to the Corinthians, chapter twelve, we are given an astonishing piece of autobiography from the Apostle Paul. God had given him an exceptional spiritual experience: he had been lifted up to the third heaven. But lest it should engender pride in the apostle, God also sent him 'a thorn in the flesh' to 'keep me from becoming conceited because of these surpassingly great revelations' (verse 7).

The world – a constant threat

Then there is the constant threat to our spiritual well-being that is posed by 'the world', with all the malign significance that the New Testament attaches to it. 'The world is ever with me, around me and within', says the hymnist. The whole outlook, mentality, and mindset of '...this present evil world...' (Gal. 1:4, KJV), is a continual menace. This is why the author of Hebrews urges his readers so earnestly at the beginning of chapter two to 'pay more careful attention...to what we have heard, so that we do not drift away.' How easy it is to just drift along with the stream of humanity, and fail to realize that we are drifting *away*. Maybe we have not fallen prey to the more obvious and overt sins of the flesh, and it is not that we solemnly decide to go back into the enemy camp. It is much more subtle than that. Forgetting that we are pilgrims on the road to eternity, we can drift away imperceptibly, almost without realizing it. Complacency and self-congratulation set in and, to use this man's illustration, we are in serious danger of being swept over the weir to apostasy and final destruction. As has often been pointed out, there is no 'marking time' in the Christian life. Unless we are positively advancing, developing, growing '...in the grace and knowledge of our Lord and Saviour Jesus Christ...' (2 Peter 3:18), we are in imminent danger of 'drifting away' altogether.

What solemn, searching issues these are – for all of us! God enable us to give them the serious attention they deserve. That is why in his infinite love and kindness, God deals with us so firmly, as well as graciously, to make us realize the urgency of these matters, and when necessary, to bring us back to himself. If only we always kept our eyes fixed on Jesus, as verse two exhorts us; if we were constantly throwing off 'everything that hinders and the sin that so easily entangles'; if we were persevering more assiduously, then so much of the chastisement we bring on ourselves would be unnecessary. But how little these things are true of us, and how inconsistent we are in the Christian race, so it *is* necessary. We need to be humbled, we need to be made patient, and above all perhaps, we need to have our hearts and minds set more '...on things above, where Christ is seated at the right hand of God.' (Colossians 3:1).

In the latter part of verse eleven we are told that the whole purpose of discipline is to produce a harvest of 'peaceable righteousness' in our lives. Here, in verses twelve and thirteen, we are given the *application* of the whole teaching.

A PRACTICAL IMPLICATION

Notice how the exhortation here is introduced, with a 'therefore'. 'Therefore, strengthen your feeble arms...etc.' If we have grasped the teaching on son-training that has been expounded to us in the preceding verses, and are endeavouring to respond rightly to discipline – then this is what must follow. Again then, the writer is reasoning with his readers, urging them to realize the tremendous implications of the teaching he has been putting before them, and apply it in practice. His argument is this: if this wonderful harvest of peaceable righteousness is only produced in those who have been 'trained' by God's discipline, and have humbly submitted to it, then demonstrate that it has indeed had its intended effect. Show it by a new spiritual resolve.

Discipline of itself is no guaranty that the recipient will *profit* by it. In his very helpful book entitled *Practical Truths from Israel's Wanderings*, George Wagner puts it like this: 'Judgments, brethren, may fall – judgments so terrible that they may make the heart quiver and bleed, and yet its besetting sin may remain as unsubdued as ever.' He adds, 'There are some persons who look at affliction as if some blessing were necessarily lodged in it...They say within themselves, "I shall be as I am until affliction comes, and then I shall be changed." This is a great mistake.'[1]

Or take this word from Spurgeon: 'Many a man has been corrected by God, and that correction has been in vain...It is not every affliction that benefits the Christian; it is only a *sanctified* affliction.' He adds, 'Take heed if God is trying you, that you search and find out the reason...Have you lost that joy you once felt? There is some cause for it.'[2]

The obvious illustration springs to mind. Those who are parents will no doubt have had the experience of reprimanding a child for wrongdoing, only to see the child *repeat* the wrong almost immediately. We do not take it very kindly when *our* children take no notice of our discipline. But neither does our heavenly Father when we ignore *his!* The point is that chastisement does not *ipso facto* produce submission and obedience. To act as if our sanctification proceeds almost automatically, while we remain passive, means we have missed the whole point of this man's argument.

Out of condition

Son-training only does us good if we submit to the disciplinary regime. The term used in verse eleven to describe that learning process is a very interesting and significant one. It is the term 'trained'. The original meaning of the word is 'gymnasium'. The authorities tell us that the root of this word gymnasium means 'to strip off'. The point is that the only people who will truly profit from discipline are those who submit themselves wholeheartedly to the training schedule that their divine instructor has drawn up for them. Think of it at the natural level. Here is a young chap who has been a 'couch potato' for much of his life. He is so out of condition it makes him puff and blow even getting dressed in the morning! Something has got to be done! So he gets himself a personal trainer. Now when the trainer tells him to get stripped off and into the gym for an initial work-out, he would be a fool if he started arguing, or complaining that exercising made his muscles ache. The whole intention in putting oneself under one of these P.E. instructors is that they know exactly what I need in order to get fit. It is a very graphic picture that we have here. The spiritual parallel is vitally important.

If we look back over our own experience, we will agree that there have been times when far from getting stripped off and getting down to the training programme that has been set us, we have made some excuse or other and not bothered to go into the gym at all.

Our Bible-reading and study have been perfunctory (if that), and our praying has been lifeless and formal. We would like to get fit (or so we *say*); we want to be blessed and have wonderful experiences, but the trouble is we would like a short cut to fitness; one that is not so strenuous and demanding as the programme that has been set us. But it will not work. There is no short cut to fitness, be it physical or spiritual. There is only one way, and that is God's way, which means that success is only attained by submitting ourselves utterly and entirely to our heavenly trainer. He alone knows what we need. The question is: Are we doing so? Or are we opting for an easier life? 'Let every man examine himself'!

A PERSONAL RESOLUTION

It works like this. Here I am in the gym, listening to the instructions being given me by my trainer. I have complete trust in him, and his programme for me. Why am I here? Where is the trouble located? What are my weak points? What needs to be worked on? Am I out of condition generally, or is there some particular area of my life that needs special attention? Have I been slacking off in the Christian life? These are the kind of questions the believer should be *constantly* putting to himself, – especially in times of trouble and affliction. Whatever the trial, the moment something untoward happens to us, we must say to ourselves: 'why has this taken place; is there a reason for it; do I need to be pulled up? Perhaps I needed a real jolt to bring me to my senses.'

Backslidden

This is how the Psalmist looked at it. 'Before I was afflicted,' he says, 'I went astray, but now I obey your word.' (Ps. 119:67). He had backslidden, perhaps almost without realizing it, but his affliction brought him up sharp; it made him think, and mend his ways. Anything that opens our eyes to our true condition, and brings us to our spiritual senses, is something for which we should thank God. With the Psalmist, we should be able to say, 'It was good for me that I was afflicted.'

Having examined ourselves and searched our motives, however painful that might be, we must honestly face up to what we find, and confess it to our heavenly Father, with no excuses. Proverbs 28:13 says, 'He who conceals his sins does not prosper, but whoever confesses and renounces them finds mercy.' And only he! In terms of the illustration here, we must admit to our trainer that we have been slack and careless, and allowed ourselves to indulge in what we call 'little' sins, as if God turned a blind eye to them.

Whatever the cost

Having done that, we must put ourselves entirely in our instructor's hands, and place ourselves entirely at his disposal. We must give him our complete attention as he spells out the training programme he has drawn up for us, and what particular exercises are needful to our condition. It may be an apology to someone; it may be we have been dabbling in something, which if not intrinsically sinful, has been a hindrance in our lives. It can be almost anything, but whatever it is, however difficult, and whatever the cost, we must do it. It does not matter how little we *feel* like doing these spiritual exercises, we must get down to them. Of course it will not be easy at first. Exercising never is to those who are out of condition! This is how this man puts it, with a quotation from Isaiah 35:3; 'Therefore, strengthen your feeble arms and weak knees...'

The trouble is, the more out of condition one is, the less inclination to do a work-out. The muscles are flabby and the joints stiff. But as any physiotherapist will tell you, what those limbs need is not rest and relaxation, but exercise and movement. What is true at the *physical* level is equally true in the *spiritual* realm. We need to keep the joints of our soul supple; we need to get down to these spiritual exercises the Scripture prescribes for us, these 'means of grace'. It is the only way to keep 'in trim', and ready for anything.

Rouse ourselves

The Bible is never feeble or sentimental over these matters. Far from encouraging us to feel sorry for ourselves when hardship and trial come, it calls for a new resolve in our lives. It treats us as adults and tells us to get on and apply the teaching. Instead of wilting under discipline, and feeling we cannot go on, we are to rouse ourselves and brace ourselves. We are not permitted to give up; this is not an option that is open to us. We must stead-fastly refuse to give way and take the line of least resistance. In effect, what our heavenly trainer is saying to us is this: 'Do not be lethargic, do not give way to apathy, and do not be half-hearted. Shake yourself out of all that. Lift yourself up, and be whole hearted in what you are doing.'

That is the secret of success at every level. In football, for example, it has often been pointed out that the player who goes into a tackle half-heartedly is frequently the one who sustains an injury. To change the illustration, you may wake up in the morning feeling tired and generally below par. But if you keep telling yourself throughout the day how poorly you are, you will feel worse than you actually are, and your work will suffer.

If on the other hand you endeavour to rouse yourself and get going, not only will you *work* better, but you will actually *feel* better. It is an extraordinary thing this, but nevertheless equally true in the Christian life. If we spent more time in brac-ing ourselves for the exercises, and less time taking our spiritual pulse, we would be far better people. So often, we persuade ourselves we are not up to anything strenuous, at least not yet; we tell ourselves that because of the pace and strain of life, we have not the time or the energy for these spiritual exercises. But look at the amount of time and energy we spend on other inter-ests! The Scripture has little sympathy for the spiritual hypochondriac. Instead of telling us we ought to slacken off and take it easy for a change, it urges us to the exact opposite. 'Pull yourself together,' it says in effect, 'get on with the exercise programme. Follow your trainer's instructions.'

When we do, the amazing thing is that it is not long before we are feeling much fitter. Even the aches and pains start to disappear. Paul exhorts the Ephesians to 'Finally be strong in the Lord and in his mighty power.' (Eph. 6:10). When we are, we will find to our great astonishment perhaps that all the power we need is given us. As the apostle puts it to the Philippians, 'I can do everything through him who gives me strength' (4:13). We have it also in those glorious words at the end of Isaiah forty, '...those who hope in the Lord will renew their strength ...they will run and not grow weary, they will walk and not be faint.'

Ultimately, there is only one way to deal with discouragement. It is to remind oneself of the truth about God. There is a great word of exhortation in Galatians 6:9: 'Let us not become weary in doing good, for at the proper time we will reap a harvest if we do not give up.' Maybe you are having a hard and difficult time. Life in this world has never been easy, and neither has true Christian living. You feel tired and weary, worn out to the point of exhaustion. But go *on*, says Paul. Take the long view. Look forward to that glorious day when you will hear those gracious words: 'Well done, good and faithful servant...'

Keep hold of the promises, and particularly the promise of special help when you need it. '...As thy days, so shall thy strength be' (Deut. 33:25 KJV), which means this: we can rely on God to give us the grace and strength required for the circumstances we are in. He is '...our refuge and strength, an *ever present* help in trouble' (Ps. 46:1).

A PASTORAL DIRECTION

Verse thirteen is part of a quotation from Proverbs 4:26. The verse in Hebrews says, 'Make level paths for your feet, so that the lame may not be disabled, but rather healed.' If the path I am taking is uneven and crooked, then any weakness in my limbs that is already there is going to be exacerbated. It might even mean a dislocation, which could disable me, and put me out of action.

What is the spiritual application to us? It means that we honestly admit to ourselves where we have gone astray. We realize afresh the need to return to the level path of righteousness; the straight and narrow way that leads to life. '...Lead me on level ground', cries the Psalmist (Ps. 143:10).

Invigorated

As we do so, seeing again the need of discipline in our lives, we find that our 'weak knees' are being invigorated, and our 'feeble arms' strengthened. It is a marvellously vivid picture. The less we *use* our spiritual muscles, the less we *feel* like doing so. As a result, our limbs grow progressively more feeble and weak, and through sheer lack of exercise, we end up as spiritual invalids. But our heavenly trainer will not allow us to sink back into apathy and inaction. He gets us back to the gym, and insists on us going again through the training programme. Thank God he does! Where would we be if he left us to our own devices, to laze away our lives in spiritual indifference and apathy?

Let us never forget that the Lord Jesus Christ has trod this way before us, and has gone ahead to 'prepare a place for us'. Let us remember always that we are in the hands of God, who will never leave us nor forsake us.

'Do not be discouraged...Let us stand together and work and pray until "the glorious morning dawns."'[3]

notes

chapter 1
[1] *Redemption Accomplished and Applied*, Professor John Murray, Banner of Truth, 1961, p.155

chapter 2
[1] *Today Thy Mercy Calls Us,* Oswald Allen, 1816-1878
[2] *Commentary on the Epistle to the Hebrews,* Philip Hughes, Eerdmans, 1977

chapter 3
[1] *Redemption Accomplished and Applied,* Banner of Truth, 1961, p.155
[2] John Murray, *op. cit.* p.152
[3] *New Park Street Pulpit, Vol. 2,* Banner of Truth, 1963, p.175

chapter 6
[1] Pickering & Inglis, 1965, p.235 [2] *Christianity & Liberalism,* Eerdmans, Reprinted 1999

chapter 7
[1] *An Exposition of Hebrews,* Baker, 1979, p.920
[2] *Collected Writings of John Murray, Vol. 3,* Banner of Truth, 1982, p.163
[3] Ibid.

chapter 8
[1] *The Christian Warfare,* Banner of Truth, 1976, p.302

chapter 10
[1] *Op. Cit.,* p.527f
[2] *Works, Vol. 1,* Banner of Truth, 1980, p.lxx

chapter 11
[1] Quoted from Philip Hughes, *op. cit.,* p.529
[2] *Thoughts on Religious Experience,* Banner of Truth, 1967, p.336
[3] *New Park Street Pulpit, Vol. 6,* Banner of Truth, 1963, p.205

chapter 12
[1] Kregel Publications, 1982, page 36f
[2] *New Park Street Pulpit, Vol. 1,* Banner of Truth, 1963, p.367
[3] In a letter to the author from Dr. Martyn Lloyd-Jones